Acknowledgments

First, we want to thank our children—Perri, Greg, Todd and Brad. Our journey through life's stages would have been greatly diminished without your presence and impact on our lives. You filled the space in our hearts and our home with your laughter, love and your God-given uniqueness. Then you moved on to create your own space with those you freely chose for life's ongoing journey. Keep growing!

Then, we want to thank the church families that blessed our lives through the years—Northside Baptist in Rock Hill, South Carolina; Harmony Baptist Church, Edgemoor, S.C.; Old Fort Baptist Church, Old Fort, North Carolina; Melbourne Heights Baptist Church, Louisville, KY.; First Baptist Church, Statesboro, Georgia; First Baptist Church, Kingsport, TN.; Interims in four North Carolina First Baptist Churches—Black Mountain, Whiteville, Wallace and Wilmington.

In all of these churches we were accepted as fellow Christians seeking to grow, serve and become more mature persons. Thank you for loving us and allowing us to love you!

I want to thank my friend, Kenan Maready, for helping me to self-publish my book. He had some expertise in this area as he had self-published three books himself: *"Chinquapin – The Way We Lived"; Chinquapin – All It's Cracked Up To Be"; and "New Hanover High School – Class of '54"*.

Following the Growth Angel

by Frank Hawkins

Contents

Introduction

On May 1, 2013, my 78th birthday, I retired as a Baptist minister. My first retirement, however, when I was almost 64, was from the First Baptist Church of Kingsport, Tennessee. I served as senior pastor of that great church for eighteen plus years. Then, after doing three interims — an intentional interim for the First Baptist Church, Black Mountain, NC; a residential interim for the First Baptist Church, Whiteville, NC; and a commuter interim for the First Baptist Church, Wallace, NC — Dr. Mike Queen, pastor of the historic First Baptist Church, Wilmington, NC asked me to serve as Interim Pastor while he was away on sabbatical. When he returned in the fall of 2004, he and the church asked me to continue serving as Minister of Pastoral Care, with a focus toward our church's homebound members. I did that for eight and a half joy- and gratitude-filled years. What a blessing!

About six months before my second retirement, my wife, Pat, and I decided to take a trip down "memory lane." She and I grew up in Rock Hill, SC. Our birthplaces were less than a mile apart in the Aragon Mill Village on Rock Hill's north side. Some of the benefits of marrying your teenage sweetheart are shared memories; they were everywhere we looked as we entered Rock Hill. We rode down Oakland Avenue and passed Winthrop University where Pat finished the last two years of college as a day student. We then passed what used to be the Pix theatre. We remembered we had our first date there at 14 and 15. The Varsity Grill was just down the street and since it was around noon we decided to go in for lunch. We looked around hoping to see familiar faces from the past, but saw none. But naturally, they would be just as "less young" as we were and not easily recognized. The Varsity was a favorite hangout for high school and college students in the forties and fifties. After years of being closed, it reopened across the street, featuring Mr. Watkins' delicious chili hot dogs which Pat and I had enjoyed as teenagers; so, we decided to try them again. They were yummy! Who says you can't eat a memory?

After lunch we rode down Rock Hill's main street—restored to some of its traditional features after being placed under a dome-like roof for some forgettable years. Our last visit in Rock Hill was to our birthplaces. We passed by Frazier Street where Pat was born. The house where I was born had been demolished. The lot is used for parking for the Northside Baptist Church, the church where Pat and I were baptized, married and where I was ordained in 1957.

There was one more memory we wanted to celebrate while in the Rock Hill area—our first pastorate and first house as a family. We took the road toward Edgemoor, a small community just a few miles from Rock Hill. That road led us to the Harmony Baptist Church, an antebellum church with a history stretching back to the 1830's. It was about 2 p.m. on a Tuesday afternoon when we stopped in front of the sanctuary. There was one car in the parking area in front of those beautiful Greek columns. The cemetery was across the road. No traffic that afternoon. The only noise was the sound of nature. I said, "Pat, let's visit the cemetery." She said, "Ok, but let's not stay long." We entered through an iron gate. The cemetery was about the size of a football field. Immediately we saw names: Nunnery, Cornwell, Collins, Reinhardt, Fudge, Simpson, McFadden, Clinton, Curry, Pittman, Mitchell, Allen, Thomas and others. We had known them, loved them, cried with them, laughed and argued with them, and made a little history with them. Pat and I stayed there long enough to laugh and cry some as we remembered past experiences with them. We were then ready to visit our first house, the Harmony Baptist Church parsonage.

The house had been built about four miles from the church in a cotton field donated by several of its members. It was about two years old when we moved in with our one year-old daughter, Perri. (Pat's dad owned a furniture store in Rock Hill and had taken us to the furniture market in High Point, NC where we were able to buy new furnishings for the house at a very good price; we were truly blessed). The ranch-style brick house had three bedrooms (one served as my study), a hall bathroom, a living, dining area, a den (with fireplace) adjacent to a kitchen and laundry room. The house was about 100 feet off the road with a lovely circular driveway to a small front porch. To us it was Shangri-La!

That day in 2013 when we arrived in front of our first family home, it no longer belonged to the church; it had been sold after a new parsonage was constructed closer to the church. Needless to say, the house was a disappointment. After all, it was about fifty years older! It also looked so much smaller; it didn't live up to our memory expectations. What went far beyond our memory expectations, however, were the three oak trees in front of the house. I remembered watering those trees during hot, dry summer days in 1961 and 1962. But then they were young and I was younger. After fifty years of growing, they had become mature, majestic oak trees.

As Pat and I finished our trip down memory lane, those oak trees became for me a metaphor for life—all life. All living things grow or have the potential for growth. This is a principle deeply imbedded in the creation itself. Pat and I have seen it at work in our lives and relationships, in the lives of our children and grandchildren. It has been visible in the lives of church members we have served, beginning at Harmony Baptist Church and continuing until the present at the First Baptist Church, Wilmington, North Carolina.

At some point in my years as a minister, influenced I know by the universal nature of the growth dynamic, a thought came to me—We live our lives in three stages. (The concept of stages is as universally known and accepted as the stages of grief; I'll write more about my dependence on this concept.) Stage one is pre-natal; we are in our mothers' wombs. That, however, is not our destiny. Then, after a brief developmental stay, we leave our mothers' bodies and begin stage two; all living human beings are stage two persons. But stage two is not our destiny either. We die and transition to stage three. There are, of course, various beliefs about a third stage. Basically there are three: one says there is no stage three; another is called reincarnation which views stage three as a recycling of life back to stage one and two. The third view is that life goes on after death in a spiritual form of various stages of growth and fulfillment.

As a human being, Christian and Baptist minister, I embrace the third view of stage three. Having lived through stage one and most of stage two has convinced me of this: the creative mind and soul behind and in all living beings connects all life stages with present and future-oriented purpose and growth. This is why I have given to this literary effort the title: *Following the Growth Angel*. In Genesis 3:24, when Adam and Eve were leaving Eden, angels were placed at the east entrance to keep them from returning. One interpretation of this pre-historical event is: Once we leave one stage of life, we cannot enter it again. The angel of growth invites us forward to the next stage. This is the way life and human history work.

This principle of growth is palpable in so many dimensions of the human experience. Agriculture and farming are totally dependent on the reliability of growth in the plant kingdom. In his parables, Jesus refers to the principle of growth as essential to an understanding of the Kingdom of God. To him, being in God's Kingdom was like being planted in good, fertile soil (Matthew 13:1-9). Teachers, in the field of education, and others who have studied and lived through the stages of life, see growth potentials in students and seek to draw them out. Our understanding of how people grow through life stages has been blessed by modern psychology. There are those, however, who tend to believe that theology and psychology are enemies. My teacher, friend and mentor, Dr. Wayne E. Oates did much to address this fallacy in his book, <u>When Religion Gets Sick</u> (The Westminster Press:

Philadelphia, Pennsylvania, 1970). Dr. Oates, professor for many years at the Southern Baptist Theological Seminary, Louisville, Kentucky, contends that all disciplines can have pockets of illness, including theology and religion. The remedy according to Dr. Oates, now deceased, is to build bridges of understanding and cooperation among the various disciplines in order to encourage health, healing and growth.

In the 1970's Pat and I had the privilege of living several blocks from Dr. Oates and his wife, Pauline. Along with being a student of Dr. Oates, I was a group leader in the Department of Pastoral Care. From his lectures, books, friendship, and Clinical Pastoral Education, I developed a perspective of pastoral ministry based on the concept of growth through life stages.

Dr. Oates, in order to undergird his own perspectives in developmental psychology, looked to other creative minds as inspiration and validation. His lectures and books were filled with quotes from Lewis J. Sherrill, Robert J. Havighurst, Victor Frankl, Eric Erikson, Martin Buber, Anton Boisen, Paul Tournier, Paul Tillich, Sigmund Freud, Karen Horney, and many others. All that he gathered from others, however, was placed on a firm foundation of belief in biblical truth as he experienced it in his personal and professional life. Pat and I learned much from my mentor, Dr. Wayne Oates, and others who have studied and lived through the stages of life.

I am now ready to share with you about the life stages through which Pat and I have lived as we have followed the growth angel. Dr. Sam Keen, a creative Christian author, once said something like this: It's important to know what time it is in your life. Dr. Keen, without a doubt, had in mind life stages through which all of us live. What stage are you in as you follow the growth angel? Come and join me as we remember, live and learn.

Childhood-Becoming an Individual Me

It is early spring – up, up and away!

Many books have been written about the stages of life. The purpose of my writing is not to examine their content. I will cite some literary works as examples to undergird my theme of sharing our experiences of moving through the stages of life. In his book, The Struggle of the Soul (New York" Macmillan, 1951), Dr. Lewis J. Sherrill wrote about the five stages of life – childhood, adolescence, young adulthood, middle age and old age (These stages occur within stage two of the three stages mentioned in the introduction). He answers Dr. Sam Keen's concern about knowing what time it is in one's life with data about the challenges of growth in each stage. The author, who gives the best clarity to the challenge of each life stage, however, is Dr. Robert J. Havighurst. In his book, Human Development and Education (New York: Longmans Green & Co., 1953), he shares about "developmental tasks." In other words, in each stage of our lives there is a growth task to undertake and complete before we move on to the next stage.

The growth task of childhood is to embrace one's own identity as a unique, different person. Let me state at this early point a conviction of mine: I believe this task which begins in childhood continues through all of life's stages. What we do and how we are impacted and influenced by parents, siblings, teachers, etc. in childhood, however, are crucially important to our identity formation through life.

As we emerge from early childhood, whether we are an only child, or one of several, we are confronted with our differentness. We are different from other family members while having similarities. A crucial question during this period for the child is: Are my differences accepted? Can I be like my family and also different? Someone has said we get our security from sameness, our creativity from our differences. I'm not sure that is always true but often it is. It was true for Joseph in the book of

Genesis. Joseph was different and that uniqueness blossomed into a very creative adulthood, in spite of sibling rivalry and hardship.

Parenting is not an easy vocation and perfection is an unrealistic goal. In homes, however, where sameness and differentness are valued and encouraged, the task of becoming differentiated according to one's own potentials stands a better chance. Dr. Paul Tournier, a Swiss doctor and devout Christian wrote a book, Secrets, (Editions Labor et Geneva, 1963) about children becoming themselves and the role secrets play in that phase of childhood development. He says children love to have their secret places (hiding places), and their secret things which they possess alone or share with their playmates. On a rainy day, when they cannot go outside, they may pull some chairs together and spread a blanket on top and enjoy their "secret place."

When I was a student at Furman University (1953-57) I visited a country church in rural South Carolina. After the worship service I was invited to lunch by one of the church's families. Their house was beautiful and the lunch was delicious. As we enjoyed the food and table talk, Mr. and Mrs. Smith's two daughters (8 and 10) began to have a private conversation in their own "secret language." I asked their parents, "What are they saying?" Mrs. Smith answered, "We don't know. They mix words in a way they understand but we can't." They were expressing their need to have their own thoughts, their little secrets as children and sisters. Their parents affirmed them; how nice! They could have said, "Secrets are not allowed in this house; just listen to us and we'll tell you what to think and how to feel." In other words, "Don't be different, don't be real persons, be just like we are." The Smith girls were getting a good message from their parents: it's ok to be different.

Childhood, of course, is a time when children need supervision and discipline. They also need the security of family sameness—rules, expectations, family rituals, etc. This does not preclude the need for freedom to explore the outreach of one's own inner creative nature and giftedness. Good but not perfect parenting seeks to listen to each child's differentness and nudge it toward its own pace of blossoming. In the story of Jesus' early development, Mary saw his differences but she didn't interfere with them. She gave him love; then, she gave him space to become, to be different. As Luke says, she just held these things in her heart (Luke 2:51).

Pat was different in her family. She was the middle child. She had an older brother, Lee, and a younger sister, Donice. Their mother, Ruby McCormick, worked away from home during most of their childhood as a successful beautician. The children were cared for by their maternal grandmother, Cora Stewart. Even though their mother and father, Carl, were away during the day, they received an abundance of love from both parents.

Discipline, during the day, however, they received from Grandmother Stewart. They knew the limits of their freedom; the only way they could leave their yard was with her presence or permission. Being raised on a farm under a strict father, Cora laid down strict rules and expectations for Pat, Donice and Lee. They had daily chores to do. Pat remembers one day when she, Donice and Lee sat down for a rest after finishing some grandmother-assigned task. Grandmother saw them sitting down and asked, "Have you finished?" They replied, "Yes, Ma'am." She responded, "Well, just stand up until I finish." They knew, though, that her "bark" was worse than her "bite." (Pat has enjoyed telling that story.)

Of the three children, Pat was the most compliant. Cora liked that and gave Pat some special attention beyond the responsible care she gave to all three. Her partiality toward Pat may have been impacted by another factor: Just as Pat was the older of two daughters, Cora had been the oldest daughter in a family of 24 children. That, no doubt, built into Cora's character a strong sense of responsibility which stayed in her as a mother and grandmother. Pat would incorporate some of her grandmother's sense of responsibility as part of her own internal parent; that would be a part, but not all, of her differentness in relating to her husband and children much later.

Pat's becoming different was also influenced by her mother and dad. I'm not sure where Pat's mother's ability to love and care came from; maybe some of it came from being the oldest daughter of her mother. Some of it, I'm sure came from a happy marriage; the love Ruby and Carl had for each other was visible — they adored each other. Pat received that love readily from her mother but felt distant from her dad. Carl was less serious and more jovial about life than Ruby. The whole family laughed at Carl's spontaneous humor. Pat, however, saw her dad as not being serious enough. She knew he loved her but experienced that love indirectly through her mother. Later, her dad's love would win her over. As a child, however, her grandmother's strong care and her mother's sensitive, loving care would shape her differentness.

Along with being shaped by environmental sources, each child has an internal uniqueness which can be cultivated but not created; it is a gift. For Pat and her sister, Donice, this was music. Their parents recognized their gifts and encouraged their development with piano lessons and involvement in church and school music programs.

While Pat was being a child in the McCormick family, I was doing the same at 4 Curtis Street in the Hawkins family. Being the last of four children made life different for me. My oldest brother, Virgil, was fifteen years older than I. He and his wife, Ruby, were married in 1938 when I was three. My sister, Katherine, was twelve years my senior. She and her husband, Bill Couick, were married shortly after World War II (he had served in the Navy).

The place of their wedding was the Northside Baptist Church. At the end of an 11 a.m. Sunday worship service, our pastor, Rev. J.J. Boone, said, "Katherine Hawkins and Bill Couick, will you please come forward now. Folks, Kat and Bill are going to get married this morning. You are welcome to stay for their wedding. But, if you have to leave, please feel free to do so now." A few left, but most everyone stayed. With only the alter flowers serving as wedding decorations, Rev. Boone officiated the wedding. Bill probably gave our pastor a two dollar honorarium for the wedding and spent an additional twenty dollars on a honeymoon to Chimney Rock, North Carolina. Things were different back then.

My other sibling, closest to me was and is Buddy. He's three years older than I. He was the older brother I wanted to be with and share the "stuff" of growing up. We did for a few years. But, then, in essence, he said, "Frank, get your own peer group." He and his buddies had a sure way to leave me behind. They would run by a poker-faced cow toward a wooded area and disappear. They knew I was afraid of the animal and would return home. It was painful at the time but turned out to be what I needed.

J.D. Ward, Dink Roof and Jimmy Sharpton became my same-age friends. Jimmy and I became what Dr. Wayne Oates called "Jonathan and David" friends. Dr. Oates observed that in late childhood, children usually develop strong same-sex friendships similar to that of Jonathan and David of Old Testament fame. This was true for Jimmy and me. We were together most every day. Some of that time was spent in our "secret place." Jimmy's dad had about twenty chickens housed in a small shed beside their home. Jimmy and I walled off a small room in the back of the shed as our hideout. In it we kept our Batman and Robin costumes. Since I was taller, I became Batman. Jimmy was content to be Robin. When we sensed danger in the air, we would enter our secret room, become the dynamic duo, and exit through a sliding door to keep the world safe from evil. Jimmy and I were expressing our need to be individuals.

My quest to be Frank Hawkins was being lived out, also, in our home. Different from Pat, I had freedom to leave our yard and be somewhat adventurous. But, at home I had a challenge. My dad, Arles Hawkins, was a quiet man. He was a responsible father. Had a good job—Overseer of the Weave Room at the Aragon Mill, and was a deacon and treasurer of our church. In my relationship with Dad there was very little "give and take." With Mom things were different. She talked incessantly. We could talk with her— even argue with her. After giving birth to four children and having several surgeries, she became overweight. Then, approaching her forties, she went through menopause. She talked to Dad, who listened but remained silent. He did not understand. None of us did. We hung on and came through it. And, in spite of the turbulence, we maintained a sense of balance as a family. Mom had her good times and gave her family much care and spontaneous humor.

So much of this happened at the family table. For example, one Saturday evening Mom prepared oyster stew for supper. Saturday night was fellowship night for us, and during the winter months occasionally we had oyster stew and fired oysters. That evening, Mom placed before us a big pot filled with piping hot oyster stew from which steam was swirling toward the ceiling. Then she left the table for a moment to get an extra box of saltine crackers from the pantry. The crackers had been in the pantry for some time. When she opened the box, a little mouse, captured inside, jumped into her individual bowl of oyster stew. As it jumped from the box to the bowl, Mom fell from her chair to the floor. After we gave the mouse a quick burial via the back door, and retrieved Mom from the floor, we had holy hilarity around the table.

Our parents do put a stamp on our identity in childhood. I embraced my mother's spontaneity. But I "boxed" it in as I also identified with my dad's reserved nature. I would deal with these life dynamics later at a more mature age. Like Pat's gift of music, however, I knew, more by intuition, that I was more than and different from my parents and siblings. I experienced it after a summer storm when I was about six years old. With the reappearance of the sun, I saw raindrops sparkling like diamonds on blades of grass. I was able, at that age, to celebrate both the storm and the sun as being good for growing things. I can also remember sitting on our back steps when I was a child. In the passing clouds I saw a parade of animals—elephants, monkeys, tigers, etc. It was the gift to imagine, a gift every minister needs.

I was different even in my appearance. My parents had dark hair; so did my brothers and sister. My hair was almost "white-blonde." My friends called me "cotton top." With my power to imagine I created a birth narrative with my being left on the Hawkins' doorsteps as an infant. Some children do create myths about the nature of their birth. I held mine on the inside until I was about eight years old.

One day I had an argument with Mom and Dad. Over what, I don't remember. The back and forth was basically between Mom and me, with Dad quietly supporting Mom. When I realized I was losing the battle, I left the room with these parting words, "I don't believe I belong to this family anyway." I retreated to my bedroom and sat down on the bed. In a few minutes I heard footsteps; they were my dad's. He sat down beside me and said nothing for an uncomfortable minute. Then he asked, "Frank, do you know the middle bedroom next to yours?" I nodded yes. He said, "On May 1, 1935 your mother was there, in bed. You had not been born. I remember her saying, 'Arles you better get Dr. Strait; this baby is ready.' Dr. Strait got here before you were born. We named you after him; his name is Frank Strait. Your hair wasn't blonde then; it was red." Then Dad said with a firm voice, "You were our son then and still are; don't ever say you don't belong to this family again."

He didn't give me a hug or say I love you. Dad continued to be by nature and nurture (I'll explain later), a quiet man, but when he did speak, his words were edifying and worth remembering. That night, at the family table, Mom's vegetable soup and cornbread had a special flavor; my birth myth was gone.

Before we move from the developmental task of childhood to that of adolescence, I need to share two other late childhood factors which helped to shape my differentness. One was a speech challenge; for several years I was a stutterer. I remember going to Mr. Onley's house with my brother, Buddy. Mr. Onley worked for our dad in the Weave Room at the Aragon Mill. He also had bees which produced an abundance of honey. Dad sent Buddy and me to pick up several jars of the honey—"a gift to our family," Mr. Onley said. When we arrived, I tried to tell Mrs. Onley why we were there; I couldn't get my words out. Buddy became like Moses' brother, Aaron, when Moses had a speech challenge before Pharaoh. I was, of course, no Moses, but I did fumble my words, especially when I became excited.

Thank goodness this problem disappeared as I moved into my teens. In late childhood, however, I wrestled with it even in my devotional life. Growing up in a Baptist church and family meant that praying was encouraged and practiced. (My family prayed—but not every day.) I prayed at night, kneeling by my bed, and after becoming horizontal. I can still hear our pastor saying, "When you pray, spend time listening as well as speaking." As an eleven and twelve year old lad, I took our pastor seriously; I did both. I never heard an audible voice. I did experience "nudges" toward good behavior and an intuitive pull toward ministry. Every time I felt that pull, however, I reminded myself and the One who was listening about my stuttering. The topic continued to be a part of my devotional conversation as I approached adolescence.

The second factor which helped to shape me in late childhood was a teacher named Blanche King. A little background: In childhood I was sick most of the time. I had a spleen which malfunctioned. I remember many visits to the doctor. My nose bled during the night; my skin had bruise splotches. Our doctor talked about delicate spleen surgery. Back in the 1940's that would have been very risky. One picture of me from that period was revealing—I looked anorexic. Suddenly, fortunately, I got better—

without surgery. I attribute my recovery to prayer and good doctors; both are agents of healing in this marvelous creation. The time I missed from school, combined with poor study habits, rendered me a "C" student. That became a part of my academic self-concept until I reached the seventh grade.

I'll never forget what happened at the beginning of that year. Miss King was my homeroom teacher at Northside Elementary School. Our first homework assignment was in American History. Miss King said, "Get out your homework, class." Then she looked at me and said, "Frank will you answer the first question?" A bolt of fear ran through my body. With a trembling voice I answered the question. Miss King walked to my desk, looked down at me and said (I'll never forget the exact words; how could I), "Frank Hawkins, that's right, that's exactly right!" I was stunned; maybe startled is the right word. No one had ever spoken to me like that.

I never recovered from Miss King's dramatic affirmation to the answer I gave that day in her History class; she jolted me into becoming a believer in me. I began to study as never before. Soon, I was making the academic Honor Roll. In the eighth grade I received the History Award for having the highest grade average in American History. I am sure there are many children in homes and schools who could use some "Miss King-like" encouragement. There are moments that help to shape destinies. I know; mine was — on a single day in the seventh grade.

Like all children, Pat and I approached the end of our childhood days. She was a McCormick; I was a Hawkins. We were ready but not entirely ready to enter life's second stage — adolescence. As we have talked about that time in our lives, Pat and I both remember being excited and afraid. We were excited about growing up — being teenagers. We were, of course, anxious about leaving some of the securities and sameness of our childhood days.

The predictabilities of Elementary school were giving way to the new challenges of Rock Hill High School. Our bodies were changing faster than our emotions. One part of us wanted to retreat back to childhood; another part wanted to forge ahead. Following the growth angel is not an easy path. Down deep on the inside we heard the call, the summons — the silent voice of nature and biology. It comes to all humankind: "It's time to leave paradise and face a world that will challenge you to evolve toward a greater maturity." The "garden of given-ness" must give way to producing your own stuff. Pat and I were not ready for the full measure of that responsibility; no one is. We were leaving paradise but not entirely. Some aspects of our lives were developing faster than others. It's very important for parents, teachers and teenagers to be aware of this truth.

I remember Dr. Oates talking about this universal principle of growth one day in class (1971, PR 158, Southern Baptist Theological Seminary, Louisville, KY). The essence of his thought was this: Growth in persons is uneven. For this reason, it is not good to compare people, teenagers especially, to others concerning their maturity. Dr. Oates asserted that a better way to think of maturity is to visualize strands or lines of development in each person. In other words, you may be more mature along one strand of maturity than I am. Along another line, however, I may be more advanced than you.

It's easy, at times, to make categorical judgments about people, or ourselves, along one strand of development and miss the other strands. As parents, teachers, and church youth workers, we can help our teenagers by affirming and encouraging them where they are maturing and, at the same time, encouraging them in areas of delayed growth. This is to see the whole person and avoid odious singular-strand comparisons between individuals. Additionally, it's possible that perceived strengths and weaknesses may turn out to be just the opposite.

There is another truth about stages I want to mention as we leave childhood and enter adolescence. It is this: There are always aspects of the left-behind stage we need to value and take with us for the unfolding journey. I believe the most crucial aspect, or trait, of childhood is spontaneous wonder; it's the power to celebrate nature and human nature as gift.

Let me illustrate: In South Carolina we didn't get much snow. When it came, I remember how we celebrated as children. We made our own sleds and played on them. Had snowball fights. Then, we would scoop up some of the white stuff and take it to Mom. She would work her magic on the snow and prepare delicious snow cream (not recommended today). I never remember our being (reflective) in our gratitude toward the divine Creator and the human creator—my mom! Our spontaneous delight and sounds of joy in consuming the snow cream were, I believe, a gift of gratitude well received by our Father and my mother. Life can stifle that kind of spontaneous wonder. Jesus told Nicodemus he needed to reach back and repossess this kind of childlikeness if he wanted to enter the Kingdom of God (John 8:1-21). It's good to know we can reach back, also, and claim it as we enter adolescence—or any age.

Frank at age 11

Pat at age

Adolescence — Becoming an Independent Me

It's late spring – I can't wait!

Everyone knows that adolescence is transitional in nature; we leave a place and move toward another. Dr. Paul Tournier presents a vivid picture of this moving process between places in his book, <u>A Place for You</u> (Harper & Row Publishers: New York and Evanston, 1968). Dr. Tournier asserts that all of us need places to be and to become; he also affirms that during our lifetime we are challenged to leave places in order to enter new ones. An analogy he uses to dramatize this truth is the image of the trapeze artist (p.163). The artist has a place which he leaves and another place as destination. There comes the moment of faith when he must let go of one bar to grasp another and swing toward the next landing in his performance.

All through life we face these times of "leaving places." The leaving we do during adolescence is not as dramatic as the trapeze act. It is, however, a time to leave, instinctively understood by most people. Some may leave prematurely and become injured by an excess of freedom. And others may play it safe and become injured by not enough freedom. The book of Genesis declares it in poetic language — we are to "leave" and "cleave" (Genesis 2:24). The leaving process doesn't have to be geographical (though often it is). It does, for sure, involve spiritual, psychological and emotional leaving or maturing. The developmental task of the teenager, therefore, a consensus view of the various disciplines, is this: to become an independent person. If the first task, that of childhood, to become an individual, is sufficiently completed, then the second task of becoming an independent individual can proceed on schedule.

Pat and I entered our teenage years in 1948-49. We were still dependent on our parents and families; we needed that security. We had become imperfect individuals influenced by good, well-intentioned parents and significant others. Our home environments, however, were becoming different. They were more like, what someone has called — "a lodge for mountain climbers." The lodge is a place for climbers to return for rest, renewal and preparation for new heights to be reached.

During adolescence, we might say, teenagers are mountain climbers. Their goal is to reach young adulthood. They go out to their world and climb. Then they return to their lodge — their homes — for rest, love, discipline and encouragement to keep on climbing. Teenagers are not obsessed with the transition which is slowly underway. They don't feel like trapeze artists or mountain climbers. They do understand the societal expectations and do feel the inaudible inner urges toward something out there beyond home and the familiar. The outward and upward thrust, however, is usually toward other teenagers — peer groups and those interesting people of the other gender. They see adults and know: "that's where we are headed."

I turned thirteen nine months ahead of Pat. We passed in the halls of Northside Elementary School, but at the time hardly noticed each other. She had a boyfriend, Marion Boling, a seventh grade classmate. In the eighth grade I had my eye on Patti Godfrey, a redhead, and Harriet Pittman, a brunette (their eyes were elsewhere). And to tell the truth — my interests were elsewhere. I had my "smoking buddies" and the Boy Scouts. That year, 1948, my family moved to the Industrial Mill Village, just about a quarter of a mile from the Aragon Village. Dad became the Overseer of the mill's weave room. Four of my classmates lived at the "Blue Buckle," the name given to the blue denim — producing Industrial Mill. They became my peer group — Don Mahaffy, Bobby Herron, Bundy McCameron, and Jerry Sutton; all of them smoked.

I yielded to the pressure and started smoking. We would go to a wooded area to do our "puffing." I guess by smoking I was declaring a bit of independence — trying to show I was growing up.

It was to become, however, an extremely difficult habit to break. But I did have fun with my smoking buddies. We brought down high-hanging mistletoe with our twenty-two rifles to sell during the Christmas season; we climbed trees to see who could carve their initials on the highest limb; we hunted, fished and cooked some of nature's produce on an open fire. We even joined the scouts together.

Our church had a scout troop — Troop 31. Don, Bobby, Jerry and I joined the troop and became members of the Black Hawk Patrol. Our Scout Master, Ed Mullis, smoked cigars and never had a rule about smoking on camping trips. There were times, I'm sure, when our pup tents appeared to be on fire. Thank goodness, later on, smoking became a medical issue. In the 1940's it was a moral issue in some churches, but not ours; even our pastor smoked. The men of Northside Baptist removed mortar between two bricks on the side of the sanctuary so the Reverend could save his "stogies" before entering the pulpit. That little indenture is still there today.

Just at the time things seemed to be going so well for my peer group, something occurred which brought on its demise. The Congress of Industrial Organizations, the CIO, led the Industrial Mill workers to strike for higher wages and other benefits. My dad was part of management. My buddies' dads were shift workers. I don't know if their parents told them to pull away from me, or, if they decided they had to do it. We never talked about it. We just drifted apart. They also dropped out of Boy Scouts. We spoke to each other at school, but our group identity was gone. It was a painful time for all involved. The strike ended when two workers placed dynamite on the front porch of one of the overseer's home. Fortunately, they were sleeping in a back bedroom and were not injured. After that act of violence, the workers slowly returned to work; the CIO had damaged itself significantly.

I missed seeing Don, Bobby, Bundy and Jerry. Entering Rock Hill High School, fortunately, gave me a new focus and the possibility of new friends. One habit, from my eighth grade peer group, I would be able to take with me to high school. Don Mahaffy, my favorite buddy, and I had learned to pole vault together. We didn't have vaulting poles at Northside Elementary. But, we decided to make our own from young, slender sweet gum trees. After cutting the trees, we would let them dry out and stiffen for about a month. Then we would jump over fences, creeks, etc. One day during the eighth grade, Don and I passed by the Rock Hill High track team while they were having spring practice. The team used our elementary school athletic field for practices. No one was practicing pole vaulting that day, so Don and I decided to give it a try. We used our own sweet gum poles and jumped over eight feet. We were thrilled when the track coach, Mr. Gene Avery, came over and said, "I want you boys to join the track team next year." I did! Don entered high school but dropped out after the ninth grade. I missed his friendship; he had potential as a student and athlete.

I entered Rock Hill High School in the fall of 1949. Mr. J.J. Godbold was our principal. He had a custom, a very good one, of reading the love chapter from the Bible—I Corinthians 13:1-13. In many ways he exemplified the meaning of the biblical text from the mind of the Apostle Paul. He was viewed, I believe, by staff, teachers, students and parents as an encourager of people. Hearing his mellow voice reading words about faith, hope, and love on the first day of classes, helped to diminish some of the anxieties about meeting new teachers and, especially, about gym classes under the supervision of Coach Walter Jenkins.

Coach Jenkins had become an institution at RHHS and in the city of Rock Hill during the '40's. He, along with the assistance from Coach "Mac" McCall and Coach Gene Avery, had led the "Bearcats" to two state football championship seasons, 1946-47. Jenkins was tough and wanted his players to be tough. Gym classes were a part of his "toughen them-up" program. I'm sure part of his motivation was to prepare teenagers for a world based on competition.

Some of his methods, however, were, I would say, somewhat exaggerated. A personal example: One day in gym class Coach Jenkins said to us ninth graders, "OK, pick a partner." We followed orders. Then he said something like, "Today you are going to box your partner without boxing gloves. You won't use your fists; you'll box with your hands open."

Coach Jenkins had been a boxer in the Navy. I guess it was natural for him to want to use that method to toughen us up. I can't remember if I chose Richard McFadden or he chose me. When our time came, however, Richard grabbed me around the neck, pulled my head down and started slapping me in the face. Then it happened. My German blood began to boil. I freed myself from his grip and charged him like a tiger pouncing on its prey. I didn't know I had that kind of power in my body; I did, and it came out.

Maybe Richard wanted to show Coach Jenkins how tough he was. To me, however, he was overdoing it. The next thing I remember was being pulled off of Richard. His nose was bleeding and one eye, which he was covering with a hand, had been hurt. Evidently Coach Jenkins was pleased. Several days later he had me to put on boxing gloves against a classmate (his name I can't remember) who had the reputation of being a good boxer. We sparred for a while but never did "mix it up." I was afraid of him, and after my bout with Richard McFadden, I think he felt the same toward me.

Inadvertently the open-hand boxing episode gave me some respect in Coach Jenkins eyes. I did not respond well to him as a coach, though. But I did respond to Coaches Avery and McCall. I was on Coach McCall's "B" Team (basketball) in the ninth grade and Coach Avery's Basketball and Track teams for the rest of high school. I guess I was demonstrating, to some degree, that I was becoming an independent person who could be a different athlete in a school where football was "King."

Becoming a sophomore meant that Pat was a freshman. I had had one date my freshman year with a blonde named Jean Kay. It was a double date with my brother Buddy and his girlfriend, Ellen Ussery. After watching a movie at the Pix Theater, we went to the Park Inn Grill, a favorite spot for teenagers to park and engage in adolescent activity. In the front seat of dad's ole' dodge there was activity; in the back seat between Jean and me there was none. I was so awkward and reserved. Jean was outgoing; I was shy. When we arrived at her home on Saluda Street, I walked her to the door. She turned and grabbed me around the neck and kissed me. I think it was a "good-bye" and "so long" kiss; we never dated again.

Pat and I started dating when I was a sophomore and she was a freshman. I really began to see her through a different set of eyes the year before. It happened at our church. After attending pre-worship classes called Baptist Training Union at 6 p.m., a group of us were standing outside before entering the sanctuary. Pat was in the group. She was laughing in a playful mood. I had seen her as a child; the child was gone. Pat, the teenager, had appeared. For the first time, I saw her new image; I liked what I saw.

Our first date came a year later. It happened on a Sunday afternoon after youth choir practice. Our church had an excellent youth choir, led by Mrs. Robinson. I joined the choir not because I had musical talent; I wanted to be where Pat was. That afternoon I had made plans with Pat's brother, Lee, to go to the Midget Grill for soft drinks. I asked Pat to go with me. Lee went with his girlfriend at the time, Carolyn Beckham. When we arrived at the Midget, it was closed. But the Esso Service Station across the street had an outside drink machine. How embarrassing! I only had twelve cents in my pocket. I had planned well for the Midget Grill (their drinks were six cents each; they were a dime at the service station). Lee bailed me out. That was the way Pat and I began our relationship.

Later that year we started "going steady." That's what we called it back then. It meant I was Pat's boyfriend; she was my girlfriend and we didn't date anyone else. It would not last throughout our high school days. But, for a while, we enjoyed the exclusive nature of our relationship. We were not married, not even engaged, but we were exploring the meaning of trust, responsible restraint, and being together in relating to family, friends and society. Those are adult-like dynamics teenagers explore before reaching young adulthood.

One part of that mutual responsibility is buying gifts for each other. In that first year of our going steady I wanted to give Pat a special Christmas gift. So, I went to a jewelry store and bought her a bracelet. Then, I did a wise thing—I showed it to my sister, Katherine. "Kat" had a way of letting you know her feelings with a facial expression. I knew my choice did not meet her approval. She said, "Frank, I don't think Pat would like that bracelet. Would you like for me to help you pick out another one?" I trusted my sister's judgment. We went back to the jewelry store and chose a Kremintz bracelet; it was dainty, with gold leaves connected to a golden rose design. It was perfect, I thought.

Let me fast forward: Pat still has that bracelet! When our daughter married Rick Miley, in 1983, she wanted to wear it. Several of the leaves were missing by then and its luster had diminished a little. I took it to a jewelry store in Kingsport, TN, where I was pastor of the First Baptist Church. "Can you restore this bracelet?" I asked. "Sure," was the response. Several days before the wedding, it was ready. "How much?" I asked the clerk. "No charge," was the reply. "It's a Kremintz and has a lifetime warranty." Wow! How surprised we were!

Adolescence is a time for learning to make decisions. It is also a time for learning to trust others who can help us to improve our decision-making skills. Katherine was honest with me and helped me make a better decision which has brought lasting joy.

The next two years were busy ones for Pat and me. We began double dating with Jimmy Hancock and Dibbie Ray. Dibbie was one of three sisters, all students at Rock Hill High. Dibbie and her sister, June, were good friends of Pat and her sister, Donice. In fact, Dibbie and June were at the McCormick's house a lot during that period. That was, however, nothing out of the ordinary. Ruby and Carl McCormick opened their home to the youth of our church quite often. We spent many happy hours there (Friday, Saturday and Sunday evenings) playing games and feeding our growing bodies with delicious, at times leftovers and at times ordered-in, food.

One day at school, between classes, Jimmy came to me and asked something like: "Aren't Pat and Dibbie Ray good friends?" I answered, "Yes." Shortly after that conversation, he called Dibbie and we started double dating. That meant using Jimmy's family car and mine on alternate dates, (during that time, most families had just one car). It also meant going to a movie, most of the time at the Pix Theatre, and afterwards to one of Rock Hill's grills — Park Inn, Midget Grill, Darlenes, Little Fields, etc. Pat and I preferred the Littlefield's Grill on Ebenezer Road. The juke box there featured our favorite dating songs, "Red Sails in the Sunset" by Tony Bennett and "Too Young" by Nat King Cole; those two singers were in their heyday. We parked, listened to music, and enjoyed each other's company with very little verbal communication.

Along with dating we were involved in school activities. Pat became a member of Ms. Guess's Glee Club. Ms. Guess was a traditionalist when it came to music. She frowned on popular music which would appeal to most young people. One day during an assembly program in the school auditorium, the rendition of a piece of music didn't set well with "Rosa B." (the name we called her behind her back). She showed her disapproval, got up from her prominent front row seat, and began to leave through a side door. Sam Mendenhall, a well-known student, opened the door for her and gave her a bow as she made her exit. The student body gave a subdued laugh as she left. Ms. Guess prided herself on teaching her musical groups the very best music. The Glee Club consistently received the highest grades possible in the state competitions held at Winthrop College each year.

To add to what she was learning from Ms. Guess, however, Pat began taking organ and piano lessons from Mr. Wheeler, a professor in the school of Music at Winthrop College. It was a wonderful opportunity for her during her sophomore and junior years in high school (Pat, her sister and her brother had taken piano lessons for many years from a local teacher). After studying with Mr. Wheeler, Pat was asked to be the organist in our home church by our first seminary-trained Minister of Music. She has one regret about that time: she convinced her mother to allow her to stop piano lessons during her senior year.

At the same time, I was heavily involved in school sports. My freshman year I was on Coach McCall's basketball team. One night I scored twenty-four points — which would be my best single night production in high school. I was thrilled when I made varsity basketball team the next year. In my first game, against a team from Columbia, South Carolina, I scored six points; not bad for a sophomore. My main sport, however, was track. I remembered Coach Avery's invitation, given when I was still an eighth grader, to join the track team the next year. I responded and was on the track team for four years. My sophomore year I placed second in the pole vault event at the University of South Carolina in Columbia, SC. My junior year I was state pole vault champion.

In my senior year we had a strong track team. We won all of our meets, including the upper state track meet at Presbyterian College, Clinton, SC. We went to Columbia that year expecting Greenville High, Spartanburg High or a team from Charleston to win; they were stronger in the track events. The meet unfolded and we were doing well in the hurdles (Jimmy Hancock won the high and low hurdle races), and the field events were going our way.

With a smile on his face, Coach Avery called us together in a team huddle. He said something like, "Guys, there's one event left and all we have to do is place in the mile relay and the championship is ours." I was one "leg" of our team in that race. We ran our hearts out for our school and placed third. For the first time in the history of Rock Hill High School — we were state champions in track! I had defended my title as state champion in pole vaulting and we took the trophy back to our Alma Mater. Even more remarkable was what happened that fall: The Rock Hill High Bearcats became state football champions. The school had two state championships in one year.

In my junior year I began to think ahead. After my senior year, where would I go to college? Am I even ready for college? These questions were mingled with a deeper consideration — what career will I pursue? I remembered, from late childhood and early adolescence, the pull I felt in my devotional life toward ministry. Those feelings had diminished but not entirely. They resurfaced as I saw college on the horizon. Being a busy high school student I had allowed my devotional life to deteriorate. In the midst of dating Pat, playing basketball, being on the track team and keeping my grades up, God and I had become strangers; the closeness I felt to the good Shepherd earlier in my life was gone. How could I be a minister for someone who was to me a stranger? The whole idea of getting up before a group of people and delivering a sermon scared me. I had flashbacks to my stuttering days.

As this kind of inner dialogue continued, I became involved in two related activities. First, I began to pray again. I would speak but there was no sense of communication. Where was the partnership I had once felt? For weeks it was that way. I shared my feelings with no one — not with Pat and not with my parents. In my family, males kept feelings on the inside. One afternoon I was home by myself. I had my nose in a book trying to study for an upcoming test. Then, I did something I had not done in years. Putting my book aside, I knelt by the sofa and said, "God, I'm not getting up from here until I get through to you." I had never spoken to God that way. What kind of response would I get? Silence? Anger? Rebuke? The response blew me away with a sense of joy. No voices. No rushing wind. There was a quiet, ineffable sense of peace. It was like an emotional and spiritual dam bursting, with cleansing waters rushing in to fill the vacuum I felt on the inside. To me, I had challenged God to be intimate and He responded — (non-verbally) "What took you so long?"

That night I was blessed to some degree, like Jacob, who at the ford of Jabbok, challenged God to bless him (Genesis 32:24-32). I have learned, however, that "breakthroughs" are never "arrival stations" to any form of perfection. My journey of growth would continue, blessed by that experience of spiritual and psychological integration. The issue of relating to the heavenly Father would resurface again later in my coming to terms with another father figure — my dad.

The second activity in which I became involved was speech. I knew whatever profession I might choose, speech would be important. This would, of course, be especially true for the ministry. So, in the eleventh grade I enrolled in Mrs. Lucy Good's speech class. Mrs. Good became my favorite high school teacher. She was short (about five feet, two inches tall), with an infectious smile and cheerful voice which created a positive atmosphere for learning the principles and dynamics of good speech. Along with writing and making brief speeches, she challenged us to write mini-plays.

I wrote one entitled, "The Last Battle." It was about an American soldier from the state of Georgia who died in a battle just before furlough time. We were at war in Korea at the time. Some in our class got excited about developing the play into a school presentation. I proved, on that occasion, however, to be too stubborn to accept script changes from fellow students; I was wrong. The play was rendered just another completed homework assignment. I did learn much from Mrs. Good, though, in the classroom and on the stage. In my senior year she invited me to take a part in the senior play. I do not remember the play's title, or the setting. My part was a supporting one. Jimmy Hancock had the leading male part. Sylvia Connor, Peggy Outen, Patsy Smith and Joanne Munn did the female parts. It was another experience of preparation for college and life beyond.

Pat and I broke up the summer before my senior year. I was the instigator (she never lets me forget). It was painful for both of us but was the right thing to do. For one thing—we were getting too serious. And, after my senior year I would be away in college. We needed, I thought, the freedom to date others. Also, after my experience of spiritual renewal, I began to think more and more about being a minister. (In retrospect, Pat and I agree: breaking up was providential for us. If we had continued to date, most likely, we never would have gotten married. As it turned out, we dated quite a few other people but never got over each other.)

During my senior year at Rock Hill High School two events, one at school and the other at church, collided and placed before me a very difficult decision. That fall I entered the Better Speaker's Tournament. The BST was a teenage activity sponsored by Baptist churches in South Carolina. Interested young people wrote speeches, on spiritual themes, which they presented in their churches. A group of adult judges selected the best speaker from each participating church for competition at the associational level, and then, at the state level. I was chosen to represent our church at the associational competition to be held at Oakland Avenue Baptist Church. The dilemma I faced was—our Varsity Basketball team had a game with Parker High in Greenville, SC that same evening.

I talked it over with Coach Avery. He thought my obligation was with the team. I was not a starter but would have played that evening. When I talked to our Minister of Youth about it, he said, "Frank, you must decide." I did decide. I represented our church in the speaker's tournament. I wish I could tell you that I won; I didn't. Andy Bass, a member of Oakland Baptist won, and represented our association in the state tournament. Our basketball team lost, also. Parker High School was a perennial powerhouse in basketball during those days. My presence with the team would not have changed the final score.

I wondered what Coach Avery's response would be to my decision. He never said a word and I played in all of the remaining games that season. I could have chosen to go to Greenville with the team; that would have been a responsible thing to do. I chose another responsible thing to do which had connections with a future beyond high school sports. The last time I saw Coach Avery he said, "Frank, I can get you a half track scholarship at Presbyterian College." He had graduated from PC and had been an outstanding member of the track team. I thanked him and told him I wanted to attend Furman University, a Baptist college in Greenville, SC. He understood.

In the spring of my last year in high school I spoke in the sanctuary of our church. The occasion was Youth Week. Most Baptist churches, true then as well as now, gave their young people the opportunity to serve in the various roles usually done by adults. This included the roles of clergy as well as lay people. Frank Lowe, a high school junior, and I were chosen by our Minister of Music/Youth, Mylus McDonald and the Youth Council, to be co-pastors. After the two Franks agreed, Rev. McDonald said, "By the way, this means you will have to share sermon time on Youth Sunday." Neither Frank nor I had ever spoken in a worship service. Then, on top of that, Youth Sunday was going to be on Easter; the church sanctuary would be filled to capacity. Part of me wanted to do it; I remembered the pull toward ministry in my devotional life. Part of me was gripped by fear; what if I "bomb out" before my family, church family and peers?

We had two weeks to get ready. I wrote my thoughts down on paper, and started practicing. Spoke to myself in a mirror. Spoke to trees in a wooded area behind our house. Spoke to my dog, Frisky. She did what worshippers probably would like to do—when she had enough she would leave. Easter Sunday came. At eleven o'clock the sanctuary was filled with people I had known all of my life. Our church was in an interim period—Rev. J.J. Boone had retired. Reverend McDonald led the service like a quarterback, calling on our Youth Week team to do their various parts; the Youth Choir sang beautifully. Frank Lowe spoke first; he gave an excellent speech. (Frank was a diligent student. Made straight A's while holding down a textile mill job throughout high school—four to twelve o'clock, Monday through Friday. Was valedictorian of his class and later became a professor in Chowan Baptist College in North Carolina.) When I stood up to speak, I was nervous. My first words were, "Brothers and Sisters in Christ, I'm scared." Everybody laughed. My mother's mouth flew open and joined the chorus of laughter. It is definitely true—laughter can send fear packing! I relaxed and felt at home in the pulpit. Gestures came—not planned—but spontaneous—appropriate to match the words being spoken. It wasn't a Simon Peter and Pentecostal moment, but it was a time of affirmation and validation for the youth of our church and for me personally. At the end of the service the church thanked us for our leadership.

Later I would remember what one of the great voices of Christianity, Richard Niebuhr, said about the call to ministry. In essence he said there are two calls: one is divine; it comes in the personal encounter between God and people. I had felt that call in the "pulls" and "nudges" in my devotional life. The other call, according to Niebuhr, is providential. In the divine call we listen to hear a summons from God. In the providential call we look within to discover gifts of mind and soul to complement and fulfill the divine call. That Sunday, in the spring of 1953 the two calls came together. I did not hear an audible voice from heaven. The voice I heard was from the church. It said, "You are a minister in the making."

In the fall of 1953 I became a student at Furman University. Pat was busy finishing her last year of high school. This included — being inducted into the National Honor Society, being chosen by the student body as a contestant in the Miss Rock Hill High School Pageant and having Jimmy Grant, a football star, as her boyfriend. At that time, I was "past history" with her. And, my attention was focused toward the "new world" I was entering.

I'll never forget that hot day in August when we arrived on campus. I had hitched a ride with Peggy Outen's dad who was driving her and her extensive wardrobe to Furman. Peggy sat in the back seat, surrounded by her stuff; all of my belongings were in a small foot locker stashed in the trunk. I sat up front between Peggy's dad and her uncle; both smoked cigars all the way to Greenville — no way to miss secondary smoke. By late afternoon I was in my new home — the third floor of Geer Hall.

A bit of history: Furman was founded in 1826. Originally it was a Men's Academy and Theological Institute in Edgefield, South Carolina. In 1850 it relocated to Greenville, SC and was named for Richard Furman, a prominent minister and president of the first Baptist convention in America. Later, the school became a private, coeducational liberal arts college. That was the case when I became a freshman at Furman.

My room was a small, unpretentious cube with two desks, pushed against two walls which partitioned off two smaller sections of the cube containing single beds and sinks. My roommate, Allen Jeffords, and I never complained. Allen was a Korean War veteran and several year older than I. I was a ministerial student; he had plans to be an engineer.

I was so naïve then—I thought all students at a Baptist college would want to pray together. So, I invited Allen to join me for evening devotional time before hitting the sack. He politely agreed. On the third evening, however, he said, "Frank, I would rather have my devotional time by myself." I said, "Sure." Allen turned his desk light off and went to bed. I had grown up in a church where young people did pray together. Allen taught me a valuable lesson: People are different and express their spirituality in different ways. That was an important realization for me to have at the beginning of my college education.

On the second day we had orientation in the chapel. Part of which was spending time with our faculty counselors. Mine was Dr. Winston Babb, who was a professor in the History Department. He and I talked about the courses I would take my freshman year, including my plans for Major and Minor subjects. I told him about my intentions to be a minister and to major in religion at Furman. Dr. Babb listened with a smile and then said something I needed to hear: "Frank, you'll get all of the religion courses in seminary. Why not take a few courses in religion here at Furman, but get a major in English or History and a minor in Philosophy or Psychology? In that way, you'll have the value of a balanced liberal arts education to add to what you will learn in seminary. I think it would make you a better minister." That was some of the best counsel I would ever receive. History became my Major; English and Philosophy became my double Minor.

The next day we started classes. It seemed that each professor asked us the same question: "What's your name and where are you from?" We, of course, answered. Then, about 1 p.m. it happened. In an ROTC class, Officer Sherman asked the same question. Gail Moul tried to answer but could not. We laughed, thinking he had a case of the jitters. He tried again but couldn't answer. We stopped laughing. Gail had a speech impediment. After the class was over, some of us went to Gail to apologize. He said, "That's ok, I'm used to it." Then, with a lot of effort, he told us why he had a speech challenge.

On December 7, 1941 he and his family were living at Pearl Harbor in the Pacific. His dad was an officer in the US Navy. That Sunday morning Gail was looking through a window of their house when the bombing of Pearl Harbor began. He saw the Japanese planes descend from the clouds. He heard the bombs exploding and was looking directly at one of the explosions. According to Gail, something in him snapped which left him speechless. After the planes left, Gail tried to talk; he couldn't. Gail's parents took him to doctors in Pearl Harbor. When they returned to the United States, they took him to specialists and received the same report, "Your son has a permanent speech impediment."

We listened quietly as Gail struggled to share with us his story. When he finished someone asked, "Gail, why did you come to Furman? What are you going to study here?" Without hesitation Gail said, "God has called me to be a minister; that's why I came to Furman." We didn't know what to say. That day, however, in the fall of 1953, that group of college freshmen became a believing community. We didn't know how Gail would be able to be a minister with his speech impediment. What mattered to us— Gail believed it. We accepted him and encouraged him and, at the same time, received his acceptance and care.

At Furman, freshman English was tough. If you made three errors on a written theme (spelling or punctuation), you flunked! I made an "F" on my first theme in Dr. Woodrow Powell's English class. I became panicky. But, instead of dwelling on the failure, I studied harder. That semester I made a "C" in English, a "B" in Speech, German and Military Science and Tactics and an "A" in Dr. Babb's History class. I was not pleased with those grades; I knew I could do better.

One day in Speech class my professor, Mrs. Sara Lowery said something which gave positive focus to my academic discontent. She said, "There is a difference between being firm and open and being firm and closed." She was referring to knowledge and religion. I had come to Furman with some knowledge about God, life and people. There was firmness in me about that knowledge. But I did not want to be closed to new knowledge which might challenge or improve the knowledge I had. That attitude, not altogether clear in my mind, would help to expand my intellectual and spiritual boundaries. In other words, as a wise person has said: "When it comes to knowledge, we need both a camp site and a horizon." If we have only a camp site, we are closed to the horizon. If we have only horizon, we lack firmness—a camp site from which to grow and expand.

Early in my sophomore year my desire and openness to learn came together; my grades improved. I became a Deans' List student. Dr. Babb asked me to grade papers for his freshman classes. Ray Austin, a ministerial student from Mt. Pleasant, South Carolina, and I became roommates. Ray was a "crossroad's friend" who became a friend for life. We studied together; were members of Furman's track team together; thumbed to each other's homes together; and made friendly competition out of most everything—shooting basketball hoops, skipping rocks across the Reedy River, etc. Everyone needs a friend like Ray Austin. Judith Viorst, a Jewish author, wrote a book entitled, Necessary Losses, (Ballantine Books: New York, 1987), in which she has a chapter on friendship. In essence she writes about various kinds of friends, i.e., convenience, common interest, historical, cross-generational and cross-roads. Some friends, however, according to Dr. Viorst, become 2 o'clock-in-the-morning friends. You just know, if you need them at that hour, they will come. Dr. Viorst claims that we don't have many 2 a.m. friends—no more than two or three.

After reading this best seller's book, it occurred to me that Jesus, also, had his 2 a.m. friends. When he went to the Mountain of Transfiguration, his time of ecstasy, he invited Peter, James and John to be with him. When He experienced his time of agony in the Garden of Gethsemane, many disciples were there. When he agonized in prayer, however, he called Peter, James and John to be near him. I have come to believe that friendship is a major if not the major theme of the Bible—God inviting his creation to share the communion of eternal community. College friendships can be "prep classes" in that direction.

1954 and 1955 were history-making years at Furman University. Frank Selvy and Darrel Floyd were back to back basketball All-Americans. Selvy scored a national record 100 points against Newberry College in 1954. As we celebrated those feats in the field of competitive sports, another dynamic, far more important, was alive at Furman. Creative minds were at work—planning and dreaming toward a new campus. The primary dreamer was Dr. John Laney Plyler, Furman's president, who led the school trustees to secure more than a thousand acres to the north of Greenville, close to Paris Mountain, with the Blue Ridge Mountains in view. Those of us who were students during that period would not make the transition to the new campus. We did, however, listen to the dream being shared by the dreamer in chapel services.

What a lesson to young minds contemplating their future—achievements begin as dreams (mental images) in courageous minds dedicated to honoring the past by giving creative leadership into the future. (If you haven't already—visit the realized dream—one of America's most beautiful campuses.)

As I finished my sophomore year at Furman, Pat was finishing her freshman year at North Greenville Junior College, located north of Greenville. NGJC was a two year Baptist institution from which students moved on to finish their college experience in four year colleges similar to Furman University. Pat was a Liberal Arts student with a major in music. Mr. Charles

Gatwood was her primary music professor at North Greenville. Under his direction, the school choir enjoyed annual spring tours in Baptist churches across South Carolina. All three of the McCormick kids attended North Greenville and were members of the choir. Pat was also a cheerleader for the school basketball team, which at that time, ranked high in the nation for junior colleges. She and I had little contact during those days. I had dated several Furman girls; she was still dating Jimmy Grant who had chosen to play football at Furman University. He had received scholarship offers from Clemson and several other schools. Furman's proximity to North Greenville probably influenced his decision.

Young Adulthood — Becoming a Choosing Me

It's early summer – decisions, decisions

Lewis Joseph Sherrill, in his book, <u>The Struggle of the Soul</u>, says that the developmental task of young adulthood is — Choosing Life's Basic Identifications. In childhood and adolescence we make some choices — ice cream flavors, Christmas gifts, sweethearts, temporary jobs, etc. But when we leave our teens we begin to face choices we alone should make; choices, according to Dr. Sherrill, which will give definition and direction to our lives going forward. These are choices for which we take personal responsibility. The growth task of childhood (becoming an individual) and adolescence (becoming an independent individual) prepare us for being choosing persons who can live interdependently in relationships freely chosen. Our basic relational identification in the first two stages of life is not a choice; it is the family of birth or adoption. Growing up is a leaving process, degree by degree, which is fulfilled in a "cleaving" to a new relational identification.

Traditionally the new cleaved-to relationship is marriage. The book of Genesis states it poetically — one is to leave the family of birth and cleave to the family of choice (Genesis 2:24, RSV, 1952). It is important to affirm, however, that the family of choice for some may not be marriage. There are human beings who choose not to marry. Their new basic relational identification may be singleness. I need only to reference my seventh grade teacher, Ms. Blanche King, a single, to illustrate my point. Another basic identification we choose is a job, profession, or calling.

These two choices, one personal, the other professional, begin to frequent our minds more often and with greater urgency as we approach our twentieth birthday. I became twenty on May 1, 1955, the month I finished my sophomore year at Furman. I was leaving my teens and entering young adulthood. My professional basic identification was determined — I had chosen to be a minister, or, as we say in "church speak," I had answered the call to ministry. Entering that summer, I wanted and needed a place to experiment and try on for size the role I was to undertake in a few years. I had followed the growth angel from childhood to adolescence. All of the growth dynamics were at work in my mind and body. A part of me wanted to hang on to the comfort and security of adolescence. The growth angel, however, at work in my psyche, was pushing me forward.

After telling my college friends goodbye for the summer, I boarded a bus bound for Union, South Carolina. Reverend Hembree, pastor of the Tabernacle Baptist Church, had sent a request to Furman's Ministerial Union for a summer youth worker—a ministerial student who could lead the church's youth in religious and recreational activities. That was my assignment—my first opportunity to lead others in a ministerial role. Reverend Hembree gave me opportunities to preach—for which I was grateful; I needed to experience the feel and pressure of producing and delivering sermons in church worship services. I also led the youth in group discussions and recreational activities almost on a daily basis. I learned that summer a lesson about people: When you have a role in their lives, or the lives of their children, and they experience you as a caring person, they will open themselves up to receive counseling and friendship.

Without realizing it, my first experience in ministry was revealing the shape my later ministry style and substance would take—that of a shepherd caring for people. Reverend Hembree gave me a lot of freedom in my role as a junior minister. I felt his trust and wanted to honor it in my various responsibilities. He modeled for me the kind of senior pastor/ministerial staff relationship I would follow in the future.

One other person truly impacted my life that summer in Union, SC. Her name was Florence Bradburn. Reverend Hembree had arranged for me to stay with the Bradburns that summer. Mr.

Bradburn was a small cloth plant owner. Mrs. Bradburn was a homemaker and a gracious, caring human being. She and I had a workable chemistry from the outset. This was only improved one night when I helped her de-flea her dog, Nellie. She was surprised a young minister would do such a thing. I had had lots of practice with my dog, Frisky. I guess she figured that anyone who would be kind to dogs might just make a good minister.

Florence Bradburn was, unwittingly, a good minister herself. On week days her home was the gathering place for a group of elderly women. Mrs. Bradburn had rocking chairs on her back porch. She and her friends would sit there, rock and drink Dr. Peppers and laugh while discussing family, church and community happenings. I was invited into their "sanctuary." Mrs. Bradburn was their friend and counselor. They opened up to her and shared their joys and sorrows. One day one of them, probably in her mid-eighties, said, "Florence, they treat me just like an old dog." Mrs. Bradburn listened with a smile, accepted her in her pain but politely stayed away from a family dynamic for which she was not responsible. She listened and was supportive without passing judgment.

By staying with the Bradburns that summer I salted away for future reference, thoughts about ministry. First, lay people do ministry in the ebb and flow of daily life. Second, in ministering to the elderly, you minister to the whole family. Third, I saw some of the principles of counseling being practiced among friends; without the atmosphere which friendly acceptance establishes, counseling rarely succeeds.

My experience at Tabernacle Baptist Church helped me to grow as a young minister. Coupled with what I had learned at Furman my freshman and sophomore years, I was eager to begin my junior year. One day before leaving Union, however, I visited the public library. I wanted to read something to prepare me for a philosophy class I would have that fall. I had heard about but had not read Plato's <u>Republic</u>. I checked it out and started reading; couldn't put it down. Plato and his philosophical foes and friends opened my mind and soul to the world of ideas. For two years I had had professors at Furman who challenged me to think for myself. That message was getting through to me.

Some of my church friends in Rock Hill had warned me that Furman was a liberal school; as such, it might turn me against my faith and church. My experience was just the opposite. In learning to think my own thoughts, inspired by some of the great minds in various disciplines (philosophy, psychology, religion, etc.), I felt more, not less, at home with my Baptist identity. The illustration I used earlier about the camp site and the horizon was becoming real for me: both would continue to co-exist as friends not enemies. I was experiencing, though, a freedom to choose and embrace truth beyond that identity, which was maturing not destroying its content. That was how I returned to Furman to begin my junior year.

At the same time, Pat was beginning her sophomore year at North Greenville. She had received a music scholarship as a freshman. Mr. Gatwood called on her to play the piano for the compulsory chapel services and other programs needing a pianist. She also traveled, at times, with several professors to churches in the Greenville area to play the piano when needed. Pat's musical skills were developing. So was her relationship with Jimmy Grant, so it seemed. That year, during the Christmas holidays, Jimmy gave her an engagement ring. Pat was surprised! Didn't know it was coming.

The next day, Sunday, I saw Pat after the morning worship service at our church in Rock Hill. I had heard about the ring. She reluctantly showed it to me. Then, I said, "Wedding bells are breaking up that old gang of ours." That night Pat had trouble sleeping. And the next morning she told her mother she could not keep the ring. It was not our seeing each other and what I said that changed her mind, Pat said. At the time she thought and I, too thought, our futures were separate ones. I had a girlfriend at Furman and, Pat, as she remembered, just wasn't ready to get married. Two days later she returned the ring to Jimmy; it was not a happy time.

Back at Furman, I had one eye on the present and one eye on the future. The present was going well for me. I had been chosen to be a member of the Blue Key, a national honor and service fraternity, and the Student Legislature, Furman's law-making part of student government. Ray Austin and I had decided to be roommates again. Ray was an outstanding student (Magna Cum Laude) and campus leader. Some of that rubbed off on me (Cum Laude). We learned the value of studying in dialogue with each other and friends like Monroe Ashley, Byron Walker, John Johnson, and Al Kinnett, etc.

We also had time for dating. Ray dated several young ladies at Furman. At the beginning of my junior year I met and started dating Evelyn Ellison, a sophomore from Concord, North Carolina. Like Pat, Evelyn was an excellent musician, singing with the Furman Singers under Dr. Dupree Rhame's excellent leadership. Evelyn's roommate was Beverly Graham from Lancaster, South Carolina. "Bev", at that time was dating Andy Bass (the same "Andy" who won the Speaker's tournament I entered in high school). During spring holidays the four of us went to Myrtle Beach for several days. We had lots of fun walking along the beach—far away from the demands of academia. Andy was planning to be a minister, also. Along with the fun we were having as young adults, the issue of choosing life's basic identifications (mentioned earlier), no doubt, was whispering in our minds. Were we walking along the beach with the person with whom we would share our futures and our ministerial careers?

As we returned to Furman, that issue was settled for Andy and Beverly; they did choose each other. Evelyn and I continued to date, but not with any degree of certainty about our future. She was busy with the Furman Singers and being a diligent student; I was busy getting ready to be Baptist Student Union co-president with Patsy Cook. Evelyn and I finished the school year with feelings for each other strong enough to merit my visiting her in Concord that summer. I drove up from Rock Hill and met her parents. The visit did not go well. Evelyn and I drove out to a grill for soft drinks. The rapport we had experienced at Furman and at Myrtle Beach was not there. I didn't feel it; neither did she. We made no decisions that night. On my way back to Rock Hill, however, I began to doubt the possibility that Evelyn and I would have a future together.

That fall, my senior year, Evelyn and I stopped dating. My thoughts and feelings for Pat had begun to resurface. In fact, they had never gone away. Since breaking up in high school she and I found a way to keep in touch. During holidays and summers, we saw each other, not on dates, but as friends. I knew she cared for me. My feelings for her were less evident, kept hidden from her and, at times, from myself. She and I both had felt romantic love for other people. She did for Jimmy Grant; I did for Evelyn Ellison. But we also knew there is a difference between feeling love for someone and being in love with someone to whom you are willing to commit your mind, body, soul and future. Pat and I were about to repossess that kind of love we had experienced at a more immature level as teenagers. The repossessing, however, would not be easy.

My senior year at Furman was Pat's junior year at Winthrop College. She had chosen to get a degree in Music Education. Pat had dated several guys after breaking up with Jimmy, but was not dating anyone seriously when I broke up with Evelyn. I was hopeful but not sure how she would respond to a "how about a date" from me. Instead of calling her, I chose to write her a letter. I don't remember how I reintroduced myself in the letter. I'm sure I didn't say, "Hi, do you remember me?" Pat would not have responded well to my trying to be funny. I truly wanted to see her again and see if she still cared for me. I told her I would be back in Rock Hill the following weekend and that I would like to see her if that was possible. She wrote back and said, "Sorry, I won't be here." She, her roommate, June Griffen, and several other North Greenville friends had planned to attend some activity being held at North Greenville.

That weekend came and I went home expecting not to see Pat. She returned from the trip on Sunday afternoon before I left for Furman. She told me (later) that as soon as she got home, she called me and said, "I'm back, if you want to come over." I had about an hour before I had to leave for Furman. I made a "bee-line" to the McCormick's house. We were awkward with each other for a while. And, for obvious reasons, did not assume our relationship as though nothing had happened. I had broken up with her. We had dated others, some on a serious basis. She had been engaged for two days. Although we had just an hour, we both knew something was happening. We made no commitments or plans. I kissed her goodbye and left. The ride back to Furman seemed shorter. I couldn't wait to see Pat again.

That fall I worked in tandem with Patsy Cook to give leadership to the various Baptist Student Union activities. That was complicated by the fact that some of our freshmen were residing at the new campus (at that time the new campus was just beginning to take shape; a decision had been made to house some of the freshmen there and run buses between the new and old campuses.) We were a University in transition and were adapting to that in BSU and in the other facets of our college experience.

On campus, especially among seniors, much attention was being given to the developmental task of young adulthood (already mentioned) of choosing life's basic identifications. The personal one (with whom will I share the future as an adult beyond my family of birth?) was being discussed and planned. Some were announcing engagements and wedding plans. Some, realizing that graduation was near, were checking out various human inventories to see if a promising candidate might emerge.

The professional or vocational identifications — Beyond Furman, what am I going to do as work in the real world? — was taking shape in two directions: Some were making plans for post-graduate studies; others were looking for employment or, already had jobs to which they would go after graduation. Ray and I had made our plans to enter Southeastern Baptist Seminary located at Wake Forest, North Carolina the following fall. Our chosen professional life identification, being ministers, didn't require us to receive seminary training; but, we considered it essential to a career of ministering to people in churches. Our days at Furman had significantly influenced us in that direction.

Choosing my professional life identification was not made at Furman; it was, however, concluded and confirmed there. By my junior year my academic standing was superior. Dr. Francis Bonner, dean of students, suggested that I might want to pursue a career in teaching. I gave it some thought but remembered my sense of call which began in early adolescence. In my senior year I chose to confirm that call to be a minister and receive the training I needed to do it well.

My other life identification, the personal one, was taking me back to adolescence as well. Pat and I had started dating as teenagers. Our friendship, however, never ended. My senior year, as I thought more about seminary and being a minister, I knew Pat was the one with whom I wanted to share that future. So, I wrote a second letter to her in which I invited her to Furman for Homecoming Weekend. She accepted. I knew that weekend would be crucially important for our relationship. Pat stayed with her brother and sister-in-law, Lee and Barbara. Lee met Barbara at North Greenville. After graduating there, he had enrolled at

Furman as a ministerial student. They lived in an apartment close to the Furman campus.

One of the big events of Homecoming, of course, was the football game for which Blue Key members had ushering responsibilities. I ushered Pat in first and found her a seat near my assigned section. She looked great in a beautiful black dress. I don't remember the team Furman played against that day, nor the score. I did my Blue Key duties but was so focused toward Pat. After the game we walked from Sirrine Stadium to Lee and Barbara's apartment. That night, after they were in bed, Pat and I sat on their sofa and talked at length. I don't remember everything we said. What I do remember is this: looking at her and saying, "I love you Pat, and I believe you still love me." That was the moment we both knew our love had endured from high school into college and would be there in our future. Our embrace and kiss marked the beginning of the rest of our lives.

I dreamed of taking Pat to the top of Paris Mountain near Greenville to give her an engagement ring. That didn't happen. The place where I proposed, however, was special. It happened on Valentine's Day, 1957. That evening we drove to the Buster Boyd Bridge, a favorite place for boating and recreation between Charlotte, NC and Rock Hill, SC. We parked in a place overlooking the water with the flickering lights of Pine Harbor visible in the distance. I gave and Pat received an engagement ring. We were so excited and could hardly wait to share the news with our families. Wedding thoughts were on our minds.

Graduation came on June 3, 1957. The ceremony took place at Greenville's Textile Hall. After saying goodbyes to classmates, Pat and I joined our families for lunch at one of the city's parks. My mother and my future mother-in-law, Ruby McCormick, had prepared the food. My brother Buddy and his wife, Warrenette, had driven from Greenwood, South Carolina to be with us for the occasion. My sister, Katherine and her husband, Bill Couick were also present. The lunch we enjoyed that day (both mothers were excellent cooks) celebrated two events: my graduation from Furman University and our wedding which had been scheduled for June 8, just five days later.

It rained on our wedding day, not enough to keep Ray and me from playing nine holes of golf. We had heard that wedding day rain was a sign of good fortune. If we could have chosen, I think we would have asked for another "sign." The weather, however, did not dampen our joy. The sanctuary of our church was filled for our 8 p.m. ceremony. The wedding participants were all in place. Mrs. Jessie Ayers, a vivacious and savvy lady—personal friend of Pat's mother and trusted church youth leader, directed every move of the wedding. Mr. Gatwood, from North Greenville Junior College was playing the organ prelude music. Six groomsmen, including my brother, Virgil, Pat's brother, Lee, Ray Austin, my college roommate and Andy Bass, a Furman classmate, were ready for the entry music. Pat had chosen six bridesmaids. Pat's sister, Donice, was the Maid of Honor. My brother, Buddy, served as Best Man. Charles Crocker, a childhood friend of mine, who later became the Minister of Music for the First Baptist Church, Asheville, North Carolina, was the soloist. At eight o'clock Mr. Gatwood played the Bridal March. Reverend Lewis McKinney, our pastor, entered the sanctuary from a side door; Buddy and I followed him to our places. The rest of the wedding party processed in. Then with a crescendo on the organ, Pat, escorted by her father, Carl, slowly moved down the aisle. She was radiant in a beautiful white wedding gown. There we were—ready for a wedding.

The sanctuary, on that evening, was hallowed ground for us. Pat and I had been baptized there. I had made my public commitment to be a minister there and, in a matter of months, would be ordained there. The choice we were making on our wedding day was blessed and enhanced by the memory of the other choices we had made in that room before God, family and friends. Pat and I do not remember much of what Reverend McKinney said to us. We knew, though, that we were committing ourselves to each other for life within a commitment I had made to be a minister. Pat was marrying me, however, not because I was going to be a minister but because she loved me as a human being. That's how I loved her, too. Ministry would be an expression of that love we vowed to each other on our wedding day.

At the end of the ceremony, Pat and I knelt at the altar for our pastor's closing prayer, followed by Charles Crocker's singing of Our Lord's Prayer. As Charles sang, Pat whispered something to me. I thought she said, "Don't worry." "No need for that now," I thought. It was a "done deal." What she said, however, was—"Don't hurry!" She didn't want me to pull her up the aisle. That little episode was somewhat prophetic—all through the years she has tried to slow down my pace of life—an achievement still in progress.

The reception was celebrated at Pat's parents' home. My scoutmaster, Ed Mullis, chose to give us a special wedding gift; he made a film of the reception with his 35 millimeter camera (I'll refer to his gift much later in this story). We greeted family members, friends, ate cake and, by ten o'clock, were in our travel clothes, ready for our honeymoon trip to Daytona Beach, Florida.

Buddy and Warrenette escorted us out of Rock Hill toward the road to Columbia. My brother was rejoicing over a bit of revenge for what I did to his car when he and Warrenette were married in 1955. He hid their honeymoon get-away car at a motel on the outskirts of Greenwood. One of Warrenette's cousins and I found it and gave it a guess-where-we're-going appearance. Buddy vowed to get even when I got married. He searched Rock Hill over and could not find dad's 1955 Chevrolet. Guess how he found out? Pat told him. She wanted the "works." I had hid the car in one of the parking lots of the Industrial Textile Plant (among two hundred or more cars). Buddy had his revenge.

After several miles of escort service, he and Warrenette waved us goodbye and we traveled on toward Columbia. We had not made reservations for that night in the Columbia area. After all, we were in our early twenties and so in love and some details were just not registering. As we approached Columbia, after midnight, Pat saw a motel advertisement sign—"Isle of Psalms Motel—5 miles." It was located on the road south of Columbia toward Daytona Beach, Florida. We went there expecting to see a beautiful place with lots of palm trees. It was a "dump!" Pat said, "we're not staying here." And I agreed. We returned to Columbia and found a nice motel. When I tried to register at the motel desk, the clerk asked--"May I see your marriage license?" I said, "I don't have one; they said we would get one later from the court house." He said, "I'm sorry, I can't give you a room." I said, "Sir, please come outside and meet my wife." When he saw the car with its honeymoon decorations, he said, "OK, come on in." I guess he thought we wouldn't do all of that for a one-night motel stay. After that episode I was glad Pat squealed and Buddy had his revenge.

We arrived at Daytona the next day and easily found a good motel. But guess what? Pat started her "monthly" the day of our wedding. She had planned for the two events to miss each other. The emotions and excitement of the wedding evidently impacted biology and brought us an unwelcomed honeymoon visitor. We were so in love, however, that we adjusted to the intrusion and had a great honeymoon.

We enjoyed Florida seafood, the wide and beautiful beach, and began learning at a deeper level how our families differed and how we would relate to those differences. For example, after our first night at the beach I said to Pat, "Honey, what would you like for breakfast. I'll get it and bring it to our room." I thought that would be a kind thing to do. Pat answered, "That would be nice." I asked, "What would you like?" She said, "Bring me a coke and a BLT sandwich and a bag of chips." I didn't say anything but I thought, "That's not breakfast food." That morning I had bacon, eggs and toast. Pat had a sandwich, chips and a coke.

It is so important for newlyweds to recognize that all families are different, including theirs. For Pat and me that recognition started on our honeymoon. It would continue when we returned from Daytona Beach. Pre-marital counseling, of course, can help in this learning process. The early days of the marriage, however, is the period when family differences begin to register as both assets and liabilities.

For the rest of that summer we lived with Pat's parents. I worked at the Industrial Textile Plant, cleaning looms with an air hose in the Weave Room. It was a dirty job, with blue denim dust filling the air around the looms. I earned about twenty dollars a week which would help to pay for my seminary expenses that fall. Pat planned to stay with her parents and graduate from Winthrop College the following spring. During that summer Pat and I visited back and forth between our two families. My mother became our greatest early adjustment challenge. The first time we spent the night with my mom and dad, Mom opened the door to the bedroom and came in (without knocking) where Pat and I were already in bed. "Do you have enough cover?" she asked. Pat was embarrassed. I said, "We're fine, Mom." The next morning Pat washed the breakfast dishes, thinking that would please my mom. Later that morning, Pat saw Mom re-washing the dishes—not a good way to make a new daughter-in-law feel accepted. Mom was a "clean fanatic." Her dishes had to pass the "thumb-resistance" test. Dad, Virgil, Katherine, Buddy and I had learned to have fun with her obsession. I still remember my dad saying to her, "Annie, you would have made a good Pharisee" (a reference to their ceremonial cleanliness). To Pat, however, it was not funny. When we were alone, she cried.

Living with parents and visiting other family members daily is probably not the best social climate in which to make early marital adjustments. Pat became somewhat disappointed with our post-wedding progress and confided her feelings with a family friend. She considered herself something of a marriage counselor to the youth of our church. Evidently she shared what Pat shared with her and my mom heard that Pat and I were having problems. Like a mother hen she wanted to intervene and help remedy the situation. In a private conversation I had with her she brought up the matter: "What's going on with you and Pat? I hear you're having problems." Without knowing it and planning it, I was about to have my first counseling session—with my mother of all people; it would be confrontational and affirming at the same time. I said something like this: "Mom, I love you and nothing will ever change that. But, Mom, Pat is my wife and she has first place in my life now. And, whatever we have to work out in our relationship, she and I can and will do it." Mom's face turned red and she said, "Well!" It was a defining moment for Mom and me. I was her youngest child. She was having trouble letting go. I had to set a boundary between her and me. She would, in time, come to accept it.

By the end of that summer the relationships between Pat and me and between our families were improving. I was learning to eat at times other than mealtimes, a practice of Pat's family, and she and Mom were beginning to accept each other. One insight we gained during that summer, which I have used in pre-marital counseling through the years is this: It is not the job of newlyweds to change and rearrange the lives of their in-laws. It is a temptation; but it won't work.

People have a right to be the way they are under their own roofs. Often a battle erupts over whose family is the good family to be followed. The truth is—all families have good and bad points. Newlyweds would do well to accept both families as having good but imperfect people. In their own space, then, they have the right to be the way they are. The battles to change in-laws and run up a victory flag over one family, is counterproductive. The couple belongs to both families with their unique differences. The parents live on in the lives of the newlyweds and will impact the family of choice. In this sense, we do marry not only our mates but the parents of our mates.

Pat and I began to accept that truth during the summer after our June wedding. When we were in our parents' homes, they had the right to be who they were. But, when we were in our own space as a couple, we had the right to be who we were. We were, in part, fulfilling the developmental task of young adulthood: choosing our new basic identification which was not free from our past. The difference, however, was—we were free to choose some of the customs and traits from each family. With that freedom we were able to laugh at some of the things which had upset us about each other's families. There were, however, other parental impact areas which would be addressed later, especially when we became parents.

Being separated that fall was not enjoyable. Pat was finishing her senior year at Winthrop. I was a freshman, again, at

Southeastern Baptist Theological Seminary in the little town of Wake Forest, North Carolina. Wake Forest College had been located there but had relocated in Winston-Salem, NC. The seminary occupied the old Wake Forest campus, offering Baptist seminary students, especially from southeastern states, a different and accessible location for their theological training. The weekly schedule was arranged (classes four days each week — Tuesday through Friday) so that student ministers could have long weekends with churches where they were serving.

That year I had the privilege of serving as interim pastor for our home church in Rock Hill. The church's pastor, Reverend Lewis McKinney and his family had moved to Carbondale, Illinois for a new pastorate. Looking back on that experience my assessment is — I was too young and too newly married for that responsibility. Weekly sermon preparation; pastoral responsibilities; being attentive to our still young marriage; keeping up with the demands of my class load; plus weekly commutes of over three hundred miles (We had purchased a 1953 Plymouth — payments of four dollars a week); made time fly by. The church, however, was very patient and we finished the year with Pat's graduation and a new pastor for Northside Baptist Church, Reverend James Deloach, a graduate of Southeastern Seminary. What a relief!

The following fall Pat and I moved to Zebulon, North Carolina, just a few miles from Wake Forest, where she took a job teaching piano and choral music in Zebulon, NC, at a consolidated school, kindergarten through 12th grade. Our home, beyond living with parents, was a one-bedroom upstairs apartment, with outside stairs. I told Pat it reminded me of one of Alfred Hitchcock's houses. It was "spooky." We never saw anyone downstairs. The price was reasonable, though, and we settled in for the year. There we were — young adults making choices for ourselves and yet, still needing guidance and counsel from adults more mature than we were.

Mr. Hicks (can't remember his first name) became one of those mature adults. He was the principal of the school where Pat taught. He wanted to meet both of us before the school year began. In the meeting he shared information and counsel focused toward Pat's teaching role. I guess he wanted me as Pat's husband to hear that data, too. Then he looked at me and said, "Can I give both of you a little advice?" Pat and I looked at each other and said, "Sure." He said, "The biggest problem our young teachers seem to have is getting over-extended with debts. I would urge you to start now learning to live within your means. I get a lot of calls from businesses where teachers owe money and start missing payments. Don't let that happen to you." We thanked Mr. Hicks and left his office. To this day, we consider his words some of the best counsel we ever received.

In a few months, Pat and I would move to Wake Forest and occupy an apartment in Johnson Hall, a three story dormitory which had been updated for couples without children. Pat said she would not mind driving the brief distance from Wake Forest to Zebulon, especially after a night when I was late returning from the seminary library. That evening she was playing piano for a dance class at the school. The plan was—I would return in time to pick her up; she didn't like going up the outside stairs to our apartment alone in the dark. That night I lost track of time—maybe it was Old Testament, New Testament or Greek—I don't remember. When I looked at my watch, I knew I was going to be late. I ran out of the library and rushed out of Wake Forest and was pulled over by a police officer. He said the usual, "Young man, do you know how fast you were driving?" I felt humiliated and he must have noticed. When I stammered trying to explain my predicament, he started hitting his ticket pad with his pen, and then he said, "Well, I'm going to let you off this time but if I catch you speeding again, you'll have to pay up." I thanked him sufficiently and became very obedient behind the wheel. Pat was waiting for me at the school, tired but not as upset as I thought she might be. But when a

Johnson Hall apartment became available that year we were delighted. We moved and had what Zebulon could not offer — campus security and fellowship with other couples. I never saw that police officer again but he has lived on in my sermons as an example of grace.

Guess what? Before the year was out, Pat and I were pregnant. In fact, all of the couples on our side of the third floor became pregnant. The pregnancy wave moved down the hall from apartment one to apartment two. We were in apartment three and kept the wave going. There was one remaining apartment where Al and Mozelle Wadsworth lived. After Pat and I verified our good news, I asked, "Al, are you going to make it a clean sweep?" Indeed they did! There was no group plan to make it a foursome. We were young newlyweds in love. The call to the parental stage just seemed to be a natural and good consequence.

As my second seminary year was winding down, we made a transition back to Rock Hill. Again, we were with Pat's parents. Our families were excited about another grandchild, especially Pat's mother. She was "rooting" for a girl (they already had a grandson). I was "pulling" for a boy, I thought. That summer I served as interim pastor for the Park Baptist Church, one of Rock Hill's leading churches. After two years of seminary training my self-confidence was growing, along with my sermon material. The church responded well to my leadership and became like extended family as Pat's due date drew near.

On July 23, 1959 I took Pat to York County Hospital in the afternoon. That evening, Pat's mother and I were in the Waiting Room. My eyes were transfixed on the labor-room doors. To the immediate left of the doors was a nurses' station, adorned with a flower vase containing a single red rose. A wall clock shared the time — twenty minutes 'til midnight. The doors opened and a nurse walked toward us carrying an infant in her arms. She said, "Mr.

Hawkins?" I said, "Yes." She said, "You have a beautiful, healthy baby girl." (I really thought Pat was going to have a boy).

Back then husbands were not permitted to be in the delivery room. My first full view of Perri came a few minutes later. Through a window with the blinds partially opened, I saw our daughter having her first bath. I knew she was a Hawkins; she was luxuriating in the water. All of us Hawkins love tub baths! As I watched our bathing beauty, Pat's mother said, "Frank, I hope you're not disappointed." I don't remember what I said. I do remember how I felt—I was one happy dad. The "boy" thing could wait.

My last year of seminary went by really fast. I had two reasons to be a commuter student. Pat and Perri were in Rock Hill and I was still serving as interim pastor of Park Baptist Church. Fridays could not come soon enough. During the week, Pat, assisted by her mother and sister, Donice (who was teaching school and still living with her folks), cared for Perri. I assumed night duty on weekends. Pat was a sound sleeper; I was not. So, I let her catch up on much needed sleep while I enjoyed nocturnal bonding with our daughter. After being on a cow's milk-based formula for several months, our pediatrician switched Perri to a soy-bean formula. The new formula didn't smell very good, but Perri thrived on it, and began to sleep better. The doctor asked us, at one point, if we knew what cows' milk was for. We said, "No." He said, "For calves." Made sense to us!

By Christmas that year, Pat and I were facing two important realities: I was jobless (Park Baptist had called a new pastor) and graduation was coming in May. Our families had been very supportive, especially Pat's parents. We were ready, and I am sure they were too, for us to be on our own. Pat and I had chosen each other and a professional path for our lives; we were ready for that to begin--but where? I remember asking that very question as I walked across the seminary campus during a January snow. The question was addressed to the One I believed had invited me to be a minister: "Lord, I'm about to graduate, with a wife and daughter and I don't have a job. Will you please help?"

Help came before I graduated in May. In some of my commutes, I had traveled with John Ryburg who was serving as interim pastor for Harmony Baptist Church, situated between Rock Hill and Edgemoor, South Carolina. John, a single guy, had served as Associate Pastor of a large Southern Baptist Church in Atlanta, Georgia until a health crisis caused him to resign. As he recovered, he decided to further his theological education at Southeastern Seminary. Harmony Baptist Church needed an interim minister and John needed a smaller church while he studied and regained his health; it was an excellent match. By the end of January, however, John was being "wooed" by a Baptist church in Smithfield, North Carolina---much closer to the seminary campus. When John accepted that church's call to be their pastor, he gave my name to Harmony Baptist. I was invited to preach at the church in March. Later that month Pat and I were visited by the church's Pastor Search Committee.

Graduation day at Southeastern Baptist Theological Seminary, 1960

The meeting took place at Pat's parents' house. Jack Barnes, Marian Cornwell and J.G. Curry represented the church. I don't remember what was said in that meeting. I do remember that Pat and I felt we were in the presence of genuine people among whom we would enjoy serving as pastor and family. The church extended a call to me to be their pastor in April. I graduated in May. Mrs. Cornwell, J.G. Curry and his wife, Grace, came to my graduation. Our prayer had been answered.

As I shared earlier, Harmony Baptist Church was an antebellum church, founded in the 1830's. Cotton fields and slave labor were visible in all directions from the church in those early days. When we arrived there in 1960, however, the slaves were gone but the cotton was still plentiful. Most of our adult members had other jobs and continued farming as a secondary source of income. A few of our members still were able to make "King Cotton" work for them economically. Speaking of cotton, the parsonage, just a few years old, had been built in a cotton field donated by several of its members. Pat, Perri and I moved into the house in late May, with our furniture. I was twenty-five. Pat was twenty-four. Perri was almost a year old at that time.

I had served briefly as interim pastor for two churches. Interims are not the "real deal," however. They are more "honeymoonish." Being a full-time pastor usually brings a honeymoon period when a pastor and his family first arrive. Honeymoons, of course, do not constitute the place where marriages grow. This is also true for the marriages between pastors and churches. After a brief honeymoon at Harmony, the real relationship began.

In one of my first sermons, an introductory message, I announced my intention to visit the church members in their homes, alphabetically by last name. One of my seminary professors suggested this as a good way to get to know the church membership. The church was small enough to render the idea practical (In larger churches, with multiple pastoral demands, this idea would be very difficult to practice). So, in June, 1960, I began my let's-get-acquainted program. Immediately I learned something about people which every pastor needs to know: When you visit people in their homes, chances are they will share some of the contents of their hearts.

For example, in one home a grandmother said to me as we were ending our visit, "Pastor, may I share with you something in confidence?" I said, "Sure you may." She said, "I'm not Bobby's mother. I'm his grandmother. My daughter had him back during the depression. She wasn't married. There were no jobs to be had around here—so, she went to New Jersey and found work. I kept Bobby and, in time, he started calling me Mom. When my daughter came home to visit, she was big sister; that's the way it's been through the years and I just didn't want you to hear about it out in the community." I thanked a loving mother and grandmother for trusting her new pastor with some intimate family knowledge. I never shared with anyone what she revealed to me. Nor did I hear a word about it from anyone in the community. People will open their hearts to their pastors; those revelations become sacred trusts to be guarded with care. By the way, her grandson and his wife were among the church's most faithful members.

In another home, I sat with Marian Cornwell, a sixty year-old daughter of the South. Marian had served on the Pastor Search Committee and was an avid home and hospital visitor. In fact, just about everywhere I went to visit the sick and grieving members, someone would say, "Marian has been to see us." I felt as though our church had an Associate Pastor in Marian. That day, as I visited with her in the den of her beautiful home, she opened up and shared her story. Her husband, "Three C" (a nickname everyone called him) had been a successful cotton farmer who owned and operated the area's only cotton gin. Right at the pinnacle of an outstanding career, Mr. Cornwell had a massive heart attack and died. Marian said she grieved for months. In fact, she became stuck in the valley of grief until one day when she read an article about grief and suffering. In it, according to Marian, the author wrote about being good stewards of our grief and suffering. She said she put the article down and said, "That's what I'm going to do — be a good steward of my suffering." Marian left her valley of grief and started visiting the lonely, grieving, hurting people of our church and community. She was a joy to know.

In another home, I sat with Jimmy and Cora Nunnery. It was about ten o'clock in the morning. As we drank coffee, Jimmy said, "Frank, do you know Pete Paquin?" I smiled (new pastors are eager to learn church members' names) and said, "Yes, he's one of our deacons." "I hate him," Jimmy said. (In that moment a telephone call to Dr. Richard Young, my Pastoral Care professor, would have been nice). I said, after a sip of coffee, "You do?" He replied, "Yes, I do." Then he proceeded to tell his new pastor that our church with the name "Harmony" was not so harmonious. It had been conflicted over the former pastor's long pastorate. Reverend E.L. Larson had been the church's pastor for approximately twenty years. Some of the members, evidently, wanted him to stay until the Lord's glorious return. Others, however, viewed their pastor as something of a surviving relic from Noah's ark. Jimmy belonged to the pastor-has-to-go group. Pete was a vocal supporter in the let's-keep-our-pastor bunch. The push-him-out group had won but lingering hostility was still present among church members. This was the current situation of the church I had pledged to lead as a Christian minister.

That day, at the Nunnery's dining table, a reconciling ministry began. Jimmy gave me an excellent opening. After telling me he hated Pete and why, he added, "I don't want to hate Pete; how can I stop hating him?" That statement was both redemptive and hopeful. My response, more intuitive than thoughtful, was, "Jimmy, do you pray?" He looked puzzled for a few seconds and then answered, "Yes, sure, I pray." I then added, "Why don't you pray for Pete. It's hard to hate somebody you pray for on a regular basis." Jimmy didn't reply. He just looked at me with a smile as if to suggest that he might consider it. I left the Nunnery's home knowing the theme of my ministry at Harmony Baptist Church would be a reconciling one, one that would encourage them to recapture the meaning of their name.

My next visit was with Mr. and Mrs. Mel Nunnery, Jimmy's parents. They lived about a mile from their son and his wife, Cora. Let me tell you about "Mr. Mel." He owned more land than anyone in the Harmony community — thousands of acres, some of which he leased to cotton farmers. In appearance, however, (other than Sundays) he looked like "poor folk." He wore a hat that looked like a leftover from the Civil War. His truck would rival the Beverly Hillbillies'. I can still see him arriving in front of the parsonage about six in the morning and depositing a bag of fresh vegetables on the porch. The first time, I opened the door and invited him in. He kept walking toward his truck, raised his right arm and said, " No thank you, us po' folks gotta' make a livin'."

One Sunday, that first summer, I called on Mr. Mel to lead in prayer. There was an eerie silence in the sanctuary. Then, in a high pitched voice, he said, "You pray, preacher." I prayed. Then I started receiving letters from male members of our church. All of them communicated the same message: "Pastor, I'll do anything for the church –cut the grass, paint walls, care for the cemetery – but don't ever call on me to pray in church." For twenty years, or more, very few lay people had prayed in public worship. I grew up in a church where many did. I was patient and encouraged our men to cultivate their prayer life.

Then one Sunday morning I called on Fritz Reinhardt to lead the offertory prayer. I thought that would be a nonthreatening context for a public prayer. I'll never forget Fritz's prayer. He prayed, "Dear God, bless Jesus for Christ's sake. Amen." Fritz unwittingly had prayed a marvelous prayer. When we think of the church as the body of Christ, Fritz had prayed for Christendom in its entirety – a big petition for such a brief prayer. I believe God smiled and accepted Fritz's prayer as He does all of our sincere but imperfect prayers. My visit with Mr. and Mrs. Mel Nunnery ended with Mr. Mel taking me to an outside storage house where he gave me one of his hanging hams. We ate well that evening.

One of our families, the Simpsons, operated a country store, located about a mile from our church. Their house was situated behind the store, with about forty acres of land, which was good for farming, fishing and hunting. One day in late August I stopped by their house for my let's-get-acquainted visit. Their son, Johnny, 12, was in the front yard pitching horseshoes by himself. When he saw me, he said, "Preacher, you wanna' pitch horseshoes wif' me?" I responded, "Sure, Johnny." Before long we had an audience – Johnny's mother, Mary, his dad, Brice and his older brother, Jimmy, had come to root for Johnny. He won. But, in my defeat, I won an invite to the Simpson table for five o'clock supper.

Mary was an excellent cook. The menu consisted of fresh vegetables – all from their garden, and apple pie, made with apples from their own fruit orchard. By pitching horseshoes with their son and breaking bread with them at their family table, I not only became their pastor but gained access to their hearts as a personal friend. I fished and hunted with the Simpson males. When our daughter, Perri, celebrated her second birthday, Mary Simpson made her a beautiful Cinderella birthday cake. And then, one day while visiting them again, Brice said to me, "Frank, Johnny has something he wants to say to you." I looked to him and said, "What is it, Johnny?" He responded, "Preacher, I wanna' be baptized." I was thrilled! After counseling Johnny about the meaning of being a Christian, we planned his baptism for the following Sunday morning. Johnny was the first, but not the last, Down's syndrome person I would baptize.

As I visited more and more in the homes of our church members, the old tensions generated by the divisive departure of their former pastor began to disappear. The members got the message that I was going to be the pastor of the entire church. Sunday school and worship attendance increased. Pat was invited to be the director of the Chancel Choir. At the same time she was the Music teacher at the Sullivan Middle school in Rock Hill. Her degree in Choral Music from Winthrop College was so useful in our church as a volunteer in ministerial service. (Many faithful church members have done the same across the centuries; may God reward them abundantly for their noble service).

Some of the choir members requested that their new director sing a solo. So, she agreed to do that one Sunday evening. I remember it well! Jane McFadden accompanied Pat on the piano. Jane was the daughter of Harmony's former pastor, Reverend Larson, and had led the choir before our arrival. She was a kind soul and could not have been more cooperative when Pat was invited to be the new director. That evening Pat came to the pulpit to sing. The pastor's chair was immediately behind the pulpit. That meant I could not see the facial response of the congregation to Pat's solo. Of course, I wanted it to be a positive experience. As she sang, I heard subdued laughter coming from some of the worshippers. My initial thought was — well, she won't sing for this bunch again! Then I discovered what was happening. It was summertime; the church didn't have an air-conditioning system; the windows were open; the narthex doors were open. A cat had walked into the sanctuary and was standing in front of the communion table. It joined Pat's solo and rendered it a duet. After the music ended and the cat was excommunicated from the sanctuary, there was holy hilarity at Harmony church. Pat told us later that the only thing that kept her going was looking at Jimmy Nunnery's face transfixed on hers in rapt attention.

Her leadership of the choir went much smoother. The group grew in numbers and responded well to her emphasis on learning elementary music lessons. The men had never been taught how to read music but became eager learners and gave themselves to serious study. Pat challenged them to sing an Easter cantata that first year and they were so proud when they presented it to the congregation. There were several solos in the piece and I was recruited to sing one of them. It was the part of Satan as he tempted Jesus in the wilderness. I'm not sure if that was "payback" for breaking up with Pat in high school or, if she just couldn't ask one of the male choir members to take such a demonic role. We got through it and the church accepted me back in my pastoral role.

When we arrived at Harmony, I noticed something very different about the seating arrangement in the sanctuary. The men sat on one side and the women and the children sat on the other side of the sanctuary. I asked why. The response I received was — it's just the way we've always done it. One Sunday I preached a sermon on family life and emphasized the importance of families doing things together. I mentioned worship as one place where that might happen. The following Sunday morning Roy and Doris McFadden and their children sat together. They led in breaking an old tradition and establishing a new one — families sitting together in worship. That change would become a part of the church's remembered history, written into recorded accounts of our years as pastor and family at Harmony church.

Our years at Harmony were brief but eventful. Our second child, Greg, was born on a Sunday morning. I took Pat to York County hospital, in Rock Hill, about six o'clock on November 12, 1961. She delivered Greg about nine o'clock. I was in the pulpit at eleven o'clock. The congregation rejoiced that their pastor's family had been blessed with a baby boy. Before we moved from Harmony in 1963, we would be pregnant again. In that year I began to receive communications from several pastor search committees. We were not, at that time, thinking about a move to another church. Why should we? The church had just agreed to adopt a unified budget approach, with tithes and offerings being given through Sunday school classes (giving improved greatly). Pat had led the church's musicians to a higher level of music appreciation and excellence. And, most of all, Harmony, once again, had become a harmonious, unified church with a hopeful taste for its future. Added to these positives was a mission project we adopted relating to a needy family in our community. Let me tell you about the McEntyre family.

They lived in an abandoned store building on the Lancaster highway, about five miles from our church. Mr. McEntyre was a chronic alcoholic. He and his wife had four children and she was pregnant again. Some of our young couples had helped them with clothing and food. When they visited, the dad would never talk to them. Their oldest child, Wanda Kay, 13, was attending our church services, being brought by some of our members. The first time I visited the needy family, a cold day with snow on the ground, there was no heat in the building. Mr. McEntyre was not there and Mrs. McEntyre, pregnant and wearing a man's robe and tennis shoes, was coping the best she could with her children. The youngest, dirty and wearing a wet diaper, hard from the cold, was sitting on a ragged sofa. Wanda Kay was in the back of the building trying to prepare food for her siblings. I gathered enough wood from around the building to start a fire in their stove. When Mary McEntyre had her fifth child, I took her to the hospital in Chester, South Carolina. After the delivery that same night, I took her back home. No insurance. Our hearts ached for the family, especially Wanda Kay. At thirteen she was vulnerable in many ways.

One Saturday Pat and I invited Wanda Kay to spend the night with us. She came and received motherly attention from Pat—a warm bath, lotions, hair care and food. The next morning I noticed Wanda Kay leaving the sanctuary during my sermon. On the inside I said, "Oh, no." Some of our choir members had been missing money from their purses left in the choir room. That morning, Earl Pittman, playing the role of church detective, caught Wanda taking the money. After the service Pat and I went to the choir room. Wanda Kay was sobbing and saying, "You won't love me anymore." We all cried. We reassured her that we did still love her. We loved her enough to know intervention measures were needed to rescue her and her siblings from a toxic and destructive home environment. While the church continued a ministry role in the lives of the McEntyre family, the appropriate Social Services personnel were brought in to deal realistically with child neglect and possible placement proceedings.

Right in the middle of these ministry challenges and initiatives, a group of strangers showed up one Sunday at the church. That's the way Baptist churches seek new pastors —they send a pastor search committee to listen to a perspective pastor in another church. I'm not sure how or from whom the First Baptist Church of Old Fort, North Carolina had heard about Pat and me. But, there they were, not sitting together as a group in order to not appear conspicuous. Most Baptists, however, catch on to that trick and can spot a pastor search committee once they enter the sanctuary—no matter where they sit. The rumors started—"Are you and Pat not happy at Harmony?" We were happy, and when I received a telephone call from the chairman of the visiting committee, I told him so—"Our church is growing and we are not interested in relocating at this time." The issue was settled--I thought.

Then I had a dream. Van Hughs, in my dream, called again and said he and the committee could not get us out of their minds and would we reconsider. I told him that Pat and I would pray about it and call him back. The dream came true. Van did call back in several days and asked us to reconsider. Pat and I didn't say yes but we didn't say no. We agreed to pray about it. And, the more we prayed, the more we began to believe the time was right to move away from our home environment (Harmony was about twelve miles from Rock Hill—our hometown). There was that inner nudge, that sense that we were being led from the familiar to something beyond. We couldn't explain it—we just felt it. I guess we could have stayed at Harmony for years and been happy there. But as Abram who was called away from home, Ur, toward the unfamiliar, Cana, we began to believe that God was calling us out toward a fulfillment beyond the grasp of our current knowledge. We finally accepted the call from the Old Fort Baptist Church as part of that move outward toward our continuing personal and professional growth. I called Van Hughes and told him that Pat and I were ready to consider being their pastor and pastor's family. We believed the growth angel was saying, "This way please."

The first time we visited Old Fort, Pat cried most of the way back home. The small town would depress most anyone in the middle of February, especially a minister's wife several months away from delivering her third child.

Old Fort had become a Southern Railroad passage town between the flat land and the assent to the higher elevations of the Smoky Mountains. Although it housed several industries, including a cloth finishing plant and a small Ethan Allen Furniture plant, Old Fort was "treading water" economically. On both sides of Interstate 40 Old Fort appeared very small and bleak. But when the pastor search committee took us on a tour of the extended community, hidden by the elevated terrain, we began to see lovely homes and a Country Club with a golf course. What sold us on Old Fort, however, were the people — they were kind, affable and full of affirming hospitality. Pat and I accepted the Old Fort church's call and we moved into their parsonage in March, 1963.

Once again Pat stayed with her parents for our third child's birth. We did not want to change doctors that close to birth-time. I processed the move of our furniture, began my pastoral duties in Old Fort and traveled after Sunday evening worship services to be with Pat, Perri and Greg until Monday afternoons. I was thrilled when Todd was born on April 15; after several weeks, all of us were together in the foothills of the Great Smokey Mountains.

Greg, Todd and Perri, April 1964, Old Fort, NC

Frank with Todd, Greg and Perri, May 1964, Rock Hill SC

Our years at Harmony and Old Fort were marked by brevity. This is not unusual for young ministers as they move through the maturing process of young adulthood and, of course, as they develop a backlog of sermon material and pastoral experience. Whether brief or extended, I contend, most pastors have a primary challenge or theme during their sojourn in each church. At Harmony my primary challenge had been reconciliation. At Old Fort it would be comfort to grieving people. This was immediately true, for example, between pastor and church. The members of Old Fort Baptist Church were still grieving over the loss of their beloved pastor, Reverend Groce Robinson. He had been an excellent pastor to the church's members—visiting them faithfully during their times of crisis and pain. Additionally, Reverend Robinson spent many hours fellowshipping with church members; they loved him for it. My challenge was, at first, to recognize and affirm their grief. I had no difficulty doing that—Pat and I still felt grief over leaving

Harmony—our "first love"; we knew how they felt. But, in accepting their grief, I knew I could not help them or myself by attempting to be like their former pastor. I decided to be myself and follow my own instincts about my relationship with them as pastor, preacher and friend.

In time they learned to love and trust their new pastor while continuing their love and appreciation for their former one. In working through that experience of institutional grief, I learned something about church people: they have expansive hearts and can make room for new ministers and their families across the years. Ministers and their families respond to this expansion of love and make room in their hearts for new churches. In that mutual expansion of love, grief is processed and church history is made.

Martha Hughes was the first church member to make an appointment with me for pastoral counseling. Martha was the sister of the Pastor Search Committee chairman. She was short, brunette and over-weight. Van had suggested that Martha come to see me. I felt somewhat awkward trying to counsel a single person in her mid-forties; I was not yet thirty.

When she entered my church study and sat down, she immediately began to cry. Then she said, "Pastor, I don't believe I'm a Christian." I answered, "Why is that, Martha?" She said, "I just don't feel close to God and I feel sad and unhappy most of the time. And I know Christians aren't supposed to feel that way. Do you think I need to be baptized?" I asked Martha if she had been baptized. She said, "Yes, but maybe I need to be baptized again. I'm not sure I really accepted Christ before my first baptism. I was so young then."

As I looked at Martha, I remembered a pastoral care class I had in seminary. Dr. Richard Young, on that day, talked about ministering to depressed people. He said it is easy to mistake depression and the way we are feeling about ourselves as the way

God feels toward us. Martha appeared very depressed to me. I decided to test reality. I said, "Martha, do you at times feel depressed?" She told me she had stopped taking her depression medication for a while and had an appointment to see her doctor that week. I did not refuse to consider re-baptizing Martha. I urged her, however, to see her doctor, get back on her medication and we would talk later. She agreed.

Several weeks later I saw Martha again. She was smiling and feeling positive about herself and her Christian faith. I could have baptized Martha and there would have been joy in the church over another baptism; that's our commission—to go and baptize people. Martha would have felt better, too—for a brief time—and then her depression would have flared up again and she would have blamed herself for feeling depressed. She was learning to live in an imperfect creation where all humankind participate, as the Apostle Paul said, in a creation groaning toward fulfillment (Romans 8:18-25). All of us, consciously or unconsciously, groan and grieve over losing our romance with perfection.

There are two sounds which will get the immediate attention of a pastor: the ringing of a telephone late at night and the sound of a siren signaling a possible crisis. One evening our home phone rang a little before midnight. Pat, the children and I were already in bed. George Ellis said, "Frank, I hate to call this late but there's been a tragedy at Mickey and Florence Johnson's house." Dr. Ellis was one of two physicians serving the Old Fort community. His wife had grown up in the Old Fort area and they had chosen to live and work in our community. "What happened, George?" I asked. "It's their daughter, Micki"; she's been shot. The police are there. The Johnsons need you, Frank. I've been with them but they need their pastor." (George and his wife, Joyce, lived near the Johnsons and had heard the shots). "I'm on my way, George."

I dressed and drove out as fast as I could. When I arrived, several police officers were in the yard. The garage light was on. The sight I saw there would become one of those mental images imprinted indelibly in my mind. The driver's door of Micki's white Pontiac was open. Her body was on the garage floor with her feet still in the car. Blood was everywhere. Micki was dead. She had been shot by a male high school student who was also the father of her baby. After the baby's birth, Micki and the baby moved in with her parents. Micki continued in high school and had gone to a basketball game that night. The father of the baby was there but left early. When Micki returned home, he was in the corner of the garage with a gun. When she opened the car door, he shot her several times.

I do not remember what I said to Micki's parents that evening. There are times when words seem to lose their power. What matters is presence. I was there—embraced them and let them know they were not alone. Henri J. Nouwen, a Catholic priest, author and one of my literary mentors, values the power of presence to transform the meaning of absence. The absence which is preceded by a meaningful presence is not empty but transformed by the memory of a past presence. Every time we come to the communion table we celebrate a past presence which our Lord commands us to remember. He "showed up" in history with a transformative presence—the cross and resurrection. Without the historical presence, the communion table would be a place of emptiness. But because He was present in the past, the communion table becomes, through mystery and grace, a place of eternal presence.

If I had not gone to the Johnsons that night, my absence would have been a barrier to the spiritual presence the Johnsons needed, and would need, to get through their hellish nightmare. But we were there—the church was present with food, prayers and visits. We were there at Westmoreland-Hawkins Funeral Home in Marion, North Carolina before the funeral. I remember talking with Mr. Sig Westmoreland, funeral director, when he looked through a window and said, "My God, the young man's car is parked outside." He had eluded the police for days but there he was—in the funeral home parking lot—dead from a self-inflicted gunshot. Again, I do not remember what I said in the funeral service. But we were there—church, community and friends. After the funeral some of us continued to visit the Johnsons—helping them to rearrange Micki's room and get ready to adopt their parentless grandson. Their grief would continue but they were not alone.

One afternoon while preparing a sermon at the church, I heard the blaring sound of an ambulance siren. In my mind I followed the route being taken by the vehicle. It was headed east on the Marion highway. The sound faded but I could still hear a faint sound indicating a northward turn. Somehow, I can't remember the details, I found out there had been a problem at a campground located on one the mountain roads. It was a popular place for campers to park their mobile homes and enjoy the beauty of the smoky mountains. I decided to go and see what help might be needed. When I arrived, I found a family from Florida in shock and grief. They (mother, father and children) had decided to take a swim in the stream which ran through the campgrounds. Their fun was interrupted, however, when the mother had left the cold water, laid down on a rock and became unconscious. Attempts were made by the husband and friends to revive her; she didn't respond. When the ambulance arrived, the crew tried to revive her; they could not. When I arrived, the father and children were sitting down, with a host of people around them.

They were, however, not alone. Someone from our church was there, and it was not me. Sam Tilson, an older dedicated layman, had come before I arrived. I saw him kneeling beside the grieving family, with his arms around them, praying in their hour of great need. His prayer was straight from the heart. He was the pastor they needed and I became Sam's assistant pastor. I knelt and listened to a human shepherd calling on the eternal Shepherd to be with a family wounded by the tragic and unexpected loss of a young wife and mother. After the prayer, Sam and I continued to comfort the family and their friends.

Again, what was most important, were not words but presence. Sam had been the presence of Christ to them and I had assisted him in communicating that presence. Several months later I received a letter from that single husband and father. He thanked our church and me for our caring ministry. Then he wrote, "Please tell Mr. Sam he'll never know how much his prayer and presence meant to us on that day."

Ministering to people during their experiences of grief can lead to life-long friendships. This was true in the lives of Robert and Jean Creekmore. Robert had moved to Old Fort to assume a staff position at the textile finishing plant. He met and married Jean, who grew up in Old Fort. When Jean became pregnant with their first child, complications set in. The umbilical cord wrapped around the baby's neck, causing strangulation and death. They grieved but did not give up on plans to be parents. When Jean became pregnant again, I was their pastor. Robert, a talented musician, had been serving as church organist. When Lenora Padgett resigned as the church's sanctuary choir director, I asked Robert to be the new director. He accepted. Pat and I became good friends to Robert and Jean, and I was with Robert in the Asheville hospital waiting room when Jean gave birth to a healthy son. The umbilical cord, once again, had presented problems, but diligent medical care had prevented a similar outcome for little Todd, the name they gave their second child. We also had a son named Todd. I'm not sure if that impacted name-giving for Robert and Jean's son or not. But this I know: The friendship which began as we shared Robert and Jean's grief and joy has lasted through the years until this very day. Robert says he wants me to officiate at his funeral. Who knows—he may play the organ at mine.

I could go on and on about grief ministry — Frank and Angie Knupp's son who died in a school bus tragedy, a bank official's death by suicide, etc. Although caring for grieving people was our primary challenge, there were other dimensions of ministry which were marked by positive growth and joy. Sunday school and worship attendance grew. And, best of all, Pat decided to use her musical gifts in starting a youth choir. There was a small group of teenagers in our church. They had never, though, been challenged to become creative and do something beyond Sunday school and worship attendance. The choir, in the beginning, was small. But, after their first presentation in an evening worship service and under Pat's competent and caring leadership, the choir took wings. Other uninvolved teenagers in our church joined the choir. Then, the choir members, so excited about the choir, invited some of their school friends to participate. Before long the youth choir, about thirty five members in number, was providing special music for our Sunday evening services, and occasionally music for our Sunday morning services.

When you reach and affirm young people, you tend to reach and affirm the parents as well. The choir grew in quality and quantity, participating in a regional festival in First Baptist Church, Asheville, NC where they sang required music for which they received excellent grades. Then, during the summer of our third year, the church rewarded them with a trip to Rock Hill, SC to present a concert in our home church and at Harmony Baptist Church. It was a time of growth and also of bonding with those wonderful young people.

A flash to the future: After I retired, Pat and I were invited back to Old Fort for the church's annual homecoming. At that time, Carolyn Early was the Music Director for the church. Back in the 1960's, she was the accompanist for the choir. She went on to Appalachian State where she got a degree in Music Education and married Greg Early. Along with being a mother of two sons, she taught in the school system in nearby Marion County. For that homecoming, Carolyn came up with the idea of getting the Youth Choir of 1963-66 back together to sing during the morning worship service.

Well, they came — from far away as Florida — about thirty of them. Carolyn and Robert shared the task of playing for the choir and Pat had such a ball directing them again. I spoke and recognized in my opening remarks Reverend Groce Robinson, whom I followed as pastor of the church. He was there with Ruby Nodine, a member of the church, who had become his wife after their spouses had died. The homecoming was an event when the past, present and future came together as a true blessing. If I understand it –that's why churches celebrate homecomings.

In August, 1966 we left Old Fort, bound for Brazil. Once again we experienced the inner nudge — that intuitive feeling that God was calling us to something beyond our present awareness. We were still young adults — in the time of life when, Dr. Louis Joseph Sherrill says, we choose life's basic identifications. Pat and I had done that both personally and professionally. We had chosen each other in marriage and, we had chosen church ministry as the context of our professional identification. But, still in Old Fort, we began to wrestle with the question of "which context of church ministry." Dr. Donald E. Super, in his excellent book, The Psychology of Careers (Harper, 1957), identifies career consciousness at each stage of life: In childhood we fantasize about careers; in adolescence and early adulthood (15 to 25) we explore different careers; in young adulthood (25 to 45) we become established in a career; middle age (45 to 65) is the maintenance stage — we have a place and usually stay with it; old age is the decline period — 65 and up — we face retirement and slowdown.

Pat and I were in the establishment stage. Both of us, as teenagers, had explored the possibility of ministry as foreign missionaries. Our home church was mission-minded and had missionaries as guest speakers on a regular basis. With that background in mind, Pat and I attended a missionary appointment service held at the Ridgecrest Baptist Assembly (located about ten miles west of Old Fort). Dr. Baker James Cauthen, executive director of the Foreign Mission Board of the Southern Baptist Convention, spoke that evening. He and his wife had served as missionaries in China. Pat and I left that inspirational service and began a process of decision-making which ended in a commitment to go as missionaries to Brazil.

Pat & Frank, 1966, appointment as missionaries to Brazil, Ridgecrest, NC

The members of our church in Old Fort were committed to missions and were very supportive toward our decision to go to Brazil. This made our grief and theirs less painful, and we parted company with mutual blessings and pledges to support one another through prayers. Being in our late twenties, Pat and I were still in the establishment phase of our lives. In going to Brazil, we would be involved in international missions. Would that become the context for our ministerial careers into our retirement years?

After saying goodbye to our Old Fort friends and to our families in Rock Hill, we flew to New Orleans where we boarded the Del Norte, a cruise ship en route to Brazil.

The Hawkins family before departing to Brazil
Rock Hill, SC, 1966

Not only were Pat, Perri, Greg, Todd and I on the ship, Pat's sister, Donice, her husband, J.D. Harrod and their three-month-old daughter, Roberta, were aboard. They were going to Brazil as missionaries, also. I really wanted to go to Germany, having had two years of German at Furman University and having German ancestors on my dad's side of the family. At that time, however, there were no requests for additional Baptist missionaries in Germany.

Brazil was different: There were requests from all three grand geographical divisions—South Brazil, North Brazil and Equatorial Brazil. Brazil was growing rapidly, inspired by Brazilian visionaries who looked at the country's vast undeveloped interior and concluded that they needed a national westward movement. Since colonial days the Brazilian population had remained primarily along the eastern seaboard, with approximately eighty percent of its inhabitants living no farther than two hundred miles from the Atlantic Ocean. In the forties and fifties that began to change. The Brazilian government led the way with a courageous decision: They moved the capital from Rio de Janeiro to the state of Goiania and built a new capital city—Brasilia. In moving the capital to the country's interior, the government was leading Brazil's westward movement by example.

Also, they made a decision to open the Equatorial region by building a new super highway to that region from North Brazil, the country's largest poverty pocket. The land along the highway would be given—squatters rights style—to the people to own and develop.

When the Del Norte arrived at Rio de Janeiro, we were entering a different world. The seasons were different: winter when the US has summer; the government was different: instead of democracy, they had a military dictatorship (during a time of revolution and political unrest in South America); their pace of life was slower: "amanha"(tomorrow—wait until tomorrow); their religious life was different: the vast majority of Brazilians were Roman Catholic; their food (lots of rice, beans, beef, salads, fruits, and coffee which was strong and syrupy) was different; and, of course, their language was different. They spoke Portuguese. Learning the language of Brazil became our immediate and greatest source of culture shock.

To learn Portuguese we moved to Campinas, an interior city located west of Sao Paulo, the capital of the state of Sao Paulo. Campinas, to us, did not appear to be large enough to boast of two hundred and fifty thousand inhabitants. But, it was true. We found out why once we moved our furniture (brought from the states) into our home. Houses in Brazil were constructed very close together on small lots separated often by a shared wall. Living, of course, in such close quarters made Brazilian towns and cities appear smaller. It was there in Campinas, that we started our quest to learn Portuguese. The Association of the School of Portuguese and Orientation, founded by American missionaries, offered classes to missionaries from all protestant denominations. We had classes five days a week, both morning and afternoon.

Perri was immediately enrolled in a Brazilian school in the first grade. She attended only morning classes, but met with a Brazilian tutor in the afternoons. Our two boys, 3 and 5 years of age, were placed in a Brazilian nursery school. They quickly learned Portuguese from school and community friends. Pat learned Portuguese faster than I did; she had studied French in high school and college and, also, was a music major which, we were told, would help in learning another language. My college German classes gave me "zero" help with Portuguese. One night we were in bed trying to "speed speak" the verb "to be" (ser, in Portuguese). It was a homework assignment. I was slow; Pat was fast. About 2 a.m., after we were asleep, some noise in the kitchen woke me up. Then, sitting straight up, Pat conjugated the verb "to be" — eu sou, tu es, ele e', nos somos, vos sois, eles sao — perfectly and rapidly in her sleep and fell back on her pillow. I thought to myself — "She's getting it in her subconscious mind and I'll never get it." But, I did — all of us did.

And our children learned the language without an accent. One day some Brazilians friends were in our home and heard our children playing with some of their Brazilian friends. They said, "If we did not know those were your children we would swear they were Brazilians."

Before we finished our year of language study, we visited the city of Americana. Our language school director, Maria Alicia, was a descendent of Americans who left the United States after the Civil War. They didn't like the way the war ended and formed a colony from various states — North Carolina, South Carolina, Georgia, Alabama, and others — and moved to Brazil. In the state of Sao Paulo, not too far from Campinas, they built a town, Americana, and started their way of life again (without slaves). With the passing of time they integrated into the Brazilian culture; some of them married Brazilians. Very close to the city, they had built a chapel where they gathered for fellowship and services of remembrance. In front of the chapel there was a monument with the names of those who had left Dixie to live in Brazil; their remains rested in an adjacent cemetery.

Then, after consuming delicious food — lunch on the grounds — a great southern tradition — we entered a chapel where I had been invited to speak. I went to the pulpit behind which there was hanging on the wall a large rebel flag. There were no rebel cries, no talk of secession — just a reminder of where they had originated. I said something like this: "Folks, I don't know enough Portuguese to speak to you as a Brazilian (we had only been in Brazil for six months), but I know you still remember some southern English. So, I'm going to speak to you in slow, South Carolina English." They laughed. I settled down. The rebel flag faded. We became church.

After a year of studying the language of Brazil, we and our fellow missionaries scattered to various parts of the country to do mission work. Some went to North Brazil. Mack and Audrey Shultz and their six children were among those, moving to the city of Recife where Mack would teach in the Baptist seminary. Pat's sister, Donice, J.D., her husband, and their baby, Roberta, moved to Equatorial Brazil and were involved in radio and music mission work in two cities — Manaus and Belem. We chose to serve in South Brazil. In fact, an opportunity came open for me to serve as a field missionary in the Campinas area. Pat and I were thrilled; we did not have to move and our children did not have to leave their school and newly acquired friends.

My assignment was to visit the Baptist churches of the Campinas Baptist Association and encourage them to start new churches in rural areas of the state. That meant I would need to work very closely with the elected moderator of the Campinas Baptist Association—a Brazilian. That could not have worked better. The moderator was Reverend Walter Cullen. Walter was a descendent on his father's side of a family of southerners who came to Brazil after the Civil War. His father had married an Italian Catholic. In a home atmosphere of tolerance and acceptance, Walter had been shaped to be a compassionate and understanding person and pastor. He received his seminary training at the Southwestern Baptist Theological Seminary in Waco, Texas. He was intelligent and goal-oriented. The church of which he was pastor had members from all socio-economic-racial categories.

In our first meeting we came up with a dream: Lead the churches of our association to start two new churches (called congregations by Brazilian Baptists) in two years. After the association adopted the goal, we identified a rural city without a Baptist presence for our first start—Capivari, a city of thirty-five thousand inhabitants. Walter and I visited the site and discovered that the only Christian presence in Capivari was Brazilian Catholicism. There had been a Presbyterian church there; it had closed its doors. How would Brazilians respond to another attempt to start a non-Catholic church?

Frank (far right) with Walter Cullen (2nd from right) meeting with a group of Brazilian Baptist ministers, 1967, Campinas, Brazil

Walter, having a mother who was Catholic, was well-versed on the subject of Catholic-Protestant relations in Brazil. Early on, when Protestants tried to start their own churches, there was rejection and persecution. In time, however, rejection and open hostility gave way to toleration. Then, as Brazil continued to develop as a participant in the world economy, its leaders, most of whom were Catholics, began to notice that in countries with a strong Protestant presence, there was also a strong middle class, i.e., the United States of America. So, wanting to encourage the growth of its own middle class, Brazil became more tolerant toward Protestantism.

This was certainly true during our time in Brazil. The government, although a military dictatorship and heavily oriented toward Catholicism, gave us freedom without hindrance to share our version of the Christian faith. At the same time, of course, we had enough wisdom not to start an anti-government movement. Walter's insight into the political, religious and economic dynamics at work in Brazil would be very useful as we moved to establish a Baptist church in Capivari.

Our plan and strategy began to unfold. First, we visited the mayor of Capivari. We wanted him and the town officials to know of our plans to give birth to a Baptist church in Capivari. The mayor was cordial and gave us his blessings. Second, not having any property in the town, we rented a building close to the city square. (Many Brazilian towns had at their center a square, beautifully maintained as a social gathering place). Third, Walter and I visited the Baptist seminary in Rio de Janeiro—O Seminario Teologico Batista de Rio de Janeiro—the oldest and largest among Brazilian Baptists' seminaries. Walter, more proficient with Portuguese, shared our dream with a gathering of the students in the seminary cafeteria.

He and I had decided to invite a small group of seminary students to help us with the church start. They would live in Capivari during their summer break. We would provide lodging (in our rented building) and meals (prepared by a few Baptist volunteers) and offer a small stipend for their ministry. They would not be involved in a preaching ministry; they would simply get acquainted with the people of Capivari and offer practical help to people in their daily activities and challenges. At the end of our visit, we had more than enough students signed up for the mission project. Fourth, we planned two Saturday evening worship services (to take place in the city square), prior to a four-day revival in a rented assembly hall.

On Saturday nights Brazilians gathered in the city square. It was the place to be. And it was the place where young people came to meet and date. They had a ritual which went something like this: The males walked clockwise around the square; the females walked counter-clockwise. If two of them became interested in each other, they would stop and talk. If a boy walked home with a girl, that was a sign their intentions were more than just casual.

We invited several of our most respected Brazilian pastors to speak at the Saturday evening services. To add a more festive atmosphere to the services, however, we invited a Latvian Baptist orchestra to provide concert-style music for the Saturday evening services. There were both Latvian and Russian Baptist churches in the state of Sao Paulo; they had excellent musicians and were very cooperative.

We had a plan in place; implementation, however, is the key to success. That, too, went well. The students became known in Capivari for their compassionate service. They helped people with their grocery shopping in the street markets and with daily personal needs (bathing and changing wound bandages for the elderly; the nearest hospital was a considerable distance away). This helped to create a positive spiritual and relational atmosphere in Capivari about our presence there. They knew, I believe, that we were not there trying to supplant the Catholic Church. We were there to minister to people spiritually, physically and emotionally. There were enough of those needs present in Capivari to keep both Catholics and Baptists busy without either being a threat to the other.

After the Saturday evening services and the four day revival, both of which were well attended, a new church was created as an extension of the Body of Christ in Brazil. Levi, one of the seminary students, became the church's first pastor. We weren't exactly like the Apostle Paul in Corinth or Rome. We did believe, though, that we were helping to create the kind of community where God's love in Christ can redeem lives and relationships.

For two years, Walter Cullen and I were colleagues in leading the Campinas Baptist Association to create new congregations. Then, in 1968, I received a telephone call from Dr. Thurmon Bryant, the director of the Faculdade Teological Batista de Sao Paulo. (The word "faculdade" — our English word — faculty — is used in Brazil to refer to a university or a school of theological training). Dr. Bryant, his wife, Doris and their children, natives of

Texas, had been in Brazil for almost a decade. Thurmon, well respected among Brazilian Baptists and the missionaries, was at the forefront of Baptist theological education in the state of Sao Paulo. The centerpiece of that endeavor was the school of theological training. Not as large as the Baptist seminary in Rio, the Sao Paulo school was growing and expanding its influence in the state of Sao Paulo and in bordering states.

A typical Brazilian Baptist Church, Sao Paulo, Brazil, circa 1967

The essence of what Dr. Bryant said to me was—"Frank, we are short on teachers. Would you and Pat consider moving to the city of Sao Paulo? You would teach New Testament and related subjects." Pat and I considered the invitation and agreed to move to a city much larger than Campinas. Sao Paulo, in 1968, had a population of eight million people. After saying our goodbyes to neighbors, friends and co-workers, we moved to one of the fastest growing cities in the world. Our new residence was spacious and beautiful. The Foreign Mission Board (now called the International Mission Board) spared no expense in making sure its missionary families were abundantly cared for in all aspects. Our children missed their Campinas friends but formed new friendships rapidly at the American School in Sao Paulo. There were, as well, a large contingency of missionary families living in the greater Sao Paulo area. Along with our new Brazilian friends, who were neighbors and new church members, we had more friends than ever. That was a blessing to us and our children.

Teaching people in their language, which they know better than you, requires patience, dedication and thorough preparation. I think I brought all three of those ingredients to my New Testament class. This meant, especially in the beginning, I had to stay very close to my prepared lectures. The class, however, more than twenty of them, appeared to appreciate the painstaking effort of an American to make clear to them the New Testament message in their own language. They carefully took notes and requested that I repeat some material they had not fully grasped.

As time passed, the class and I moved from a formal to a more informal relationship. I became more spontaneous in my lectures and the students felt freer to make comments and ask questions. The class was very affirming about the quality of my lectures. Some missionary professors, evidently, had lectured to them in an unknown language somewhere between Portuguese and English.

I taught several other classes while serving at the Baptist school in Sao Paulo. One was on the New Testament book of Hebrews. One night after the class, a lawyer who was also a pastor, came to me and said, "Pastor Frank, nesta noite o irmao foi bem Brazileiro." He paid me a complement every missionary loves to hear—"Tonight you sounded like one of us."

Frank teaching a group of Brazilian seminarians as Dr. Winston Crawley from Foreign Mission board looks on, Sao Paulo, Brazil, circa 1968

Dr. Bryant enjoyed teaching at the Faculdade but spent most of his time dealing with administrative issues in his role as director. I remember a school staff meeting in which he revealed to us a painful decision he had made. It involved the student workers in the school cafeteria. Because most of the students had daytime jobs, all classes were held at night. Some, however, lived on campus and helped to operate a kitchen and dining hall which provided evening meals for students and professors. Their work served as a scholarship which made affordable their theological training. The funds, Dr. Bryant shared with us, were not available to continue the scholarships. This meant the cafeteria would have to close and the student workers would drop out of school. He had sought emergency funding from the Sao Paulo Baptist Convention but was told that in an inflationary economy no funds were available. The bad news would be shared with the students in several days. We left the meeting in a sad mood.

The next day Pat and I received a letter from the First Baptist Church of Old Fort, North Carolina. In it there was a message: "We wanted you to know we haven't forgotten you and thought you could use this check in your mission work." The check amounted to five thousand dollars. That may not seem much to you, but in 1969 in Brazil it was huge! I took it to Dr. Bryant's office and said, "Thurmon, can you use this?" He looked at the check, smiled, and said — "This means the cafeteria will stay open." When he shared the good news with the teaching staff and the student body, there was rejoicing up and down the halls of the Faculdade. The students had already heard about the impending closure of the cafeteria. That evening meal had a special flavor to it — almost sacramental. Churches never know what their generosity may produce; the school cafeteria continued to exist.

Our daughter, Perri, reached her tenth birthday while we were in Brazil. We were not surprised when she came to us one night and said she had accepted Christ and wanted to be baptized. After we talked to her about her decision, we shared with our pastor, Dr. Ruben Lopez, her desire to be baptized. Dr. Lopez was a lawyer, and also, pastor of the Villa Mariana Baptist Church in Sao Paulo. He expressed his support and invited us and Perri to a baptism-preparation class. We attended and discovered that the meeting was really a testimony service. Dr. Lopez presided and invited parents to give evidence that their children were ready for Christian baptism. It was a new experience for us. Pat and I, of course, were pleased to share with the group our belief in Perri's readiness to experience Christian baptism. We were surprised, though, when a Brazilian mother testified against her daughter. She said her daughter gave no evidence at home of the kind of conduct that warrants her being baptized. After that meeting, Perri was baptized; the Brazilian girl was not.

Pat and I had mixed feelings about the baptism-preparation class. A little girl was rejected in a public setting; that was not good. Parental involvement was appropriate. It should have been, however, we believe, in a private setting at the parents' requests and with their affirmation and support.

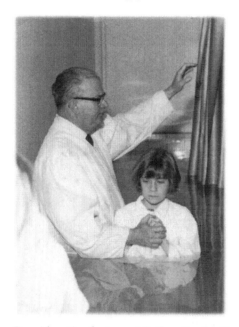

Perri baptized at age 10, Sao Paulo, Brazil

Perri, Greg and Todd enjoyed playing with their Brazilian church friends. But they had Brazilian friends who were also Catholic. In fact, their best Brazilian friends were Catholic. Alfredo and his sister, Regina, lived down the street from us. They and our three were together just about every day. One day they were playing in a field behind our house. It was a straw field and they had constructed a secret hideout there with sticks and straw. Suddenly Pat and I heard the word—"fire." Our three came running into our house wide-eyed and saying, "the field is on fire!" I rushed outside and looked. There was a brush fire. But, fortunately, the wind was a non-factor and we rescued the field and the hideout with little damage being done. We never discovered among the five friends which one started the fire. They all took responsibility for the mini-disaster.

That did not mean there was no room for anger among friends. One day they were playing soccer in front of our house. They were, no doubt, imagining they were like Pele, the great Brazilian soccer star who had led Brazil to its third World Cup victory. In their enthusiasm and competiveness, Greg and Alfredo became angry and got into a fistfight. Greg came home crying and told us he would never play with Alfredo again. Alfredo went home crying and said the same about Greg. Alfredo's dad told me several days later about a note Alfredo wrote to himself and placed beside his bed the night after the fight. He wrote, (in Portuguese, of course), "Remember, you can't play with Greg anymore. You are angry with him." The next day Alfredo's dad and I saw Greg and Alfredo chasing the soccer ball again. The note had done no good. Their friendship was stronger than their anger.

1969 was a pivotal year for us in Brazil. As we celebrated our native country's placing astronauts on the moon (our Brazilian friends celebrated, too), we began to make preparations for a year of furlough in the United States. We had been in Brazil for almost five years. What would we do with a whole year back in the states? Pat and I began to do some serious thinking and praying. We were still young adults. We had served in two churches and had been missionaries in another country. In just a few years we would be moving into our middle-age years. We had followed the growth angel through young adulthood but, in my soul, I did not feel ready for the next stage.

I felt that way personally. Part of this was my over-identification with my dad. He was one of the best men I had known. But he was a quiet, solemn person. When I was a teenager, some of my friends said, "Frank, you are just like your dad, and you even look like him." Emotionally I ran from that comparison. Dad had become an orphan as a child. His parents and only sibling, a brother, had died by his seventh birthday. Grandparents and aunts raised him to be a responsible young man. He missed, however, having the warmth of mother love; his mother died shortly after his birth. I experienced the lack of warmth in my relationship with Dad and internalized it as part of my self-image. One day, all alone in our home in Brazil, I remember shouting— "orphan." It was a moment of truth for me. I needed help to deal with my past still alive in the present. There is no way, to be clear, to separate the personal from the professional when it comes to being an effective minister. I had been an adequate pastor in the United States and a responsible missionary in Brazil as a new church starter and teacher. That wasn't enough. I wanted and needed to grow both personally and professionally.

Pat and I talked it over, and after a conversation with Dr. Winston Crawly from the mission board during one of his visits to Brazil, decided that Southern Seminary in Louisville, Kentucky was the best fit for us. I had heard of the school's excellent department of pastoral care, with Dr. Wayne E. Oates as its director. I would enroll there as a Master of Theology degree student, and, in our return to Brazil, would teach Brazilian Baptist pastors courses in pastoral care. Dr. Bryant was very affirming about our decision. Our furlough had a plan.

After saying goodbye to our colleagues and Brazilian friends, we traveled by plane from Sao Paulo to Belem in Equatorial Brazil for a week's visit with Pat's sister, Donice, JD and their daughter, Roberta. Our next stop was Miami, Florida. Our children were amazed at all of the coin machines in the airport terminal. Perri, Greg and Todd depleted our coin supply, stocking up on American candy. The following morning we ate breakfast in one of the airport restaurants. We had a good laugh when Todd, 8, ordered buttermilk for his beverage. For almost five years, he had heard me saying—"I can't wait 'til I get some corn bread and buttermilk." After a quick lesson on the appropriate time for buttermilk consumption, Todd said, "Oh well, I'll have chocolate milk."

That afternoon we met our American families at the airport in Charlotte, North Carolina. It was Thanksgiving week, 1970. Pat, the children and I traveled in different family members' cars from the airport to Rock Hill, SC (just 20 miles away). The ride itself provided some culture shock in reverse. In the city of Sao Paulo the traffic was loud and unpredictable. From Charlotte to Rock Hill it was predictable and very quiet. That year we had two Thanksgiving meals—one, that evening at Ruby and Carl McCormick house, our children's maternal grandparents' home, and, then, on Thanksgiving day at Anne and Arles Hawkins home, their paternal grandparents' home. The food was delicious; being home with our families after almost five years in Brazil was even more delicious.

In early January, 1971, after moving into a residence for furloughing missionaries at the Southern Baptist Theological Seminary in Louisville, Kentucky, Pat and I met with Dr. Wayne E. Oates in his seminary office. His desk was against the wall; his chair was positioned between the desk and visitors' chairs. His entire body was focused toward us; he listened intently to our furlough plans and encouraged me not only to take classes in pastoral care but to pursue Clinical Pastoral Education training as well. After that affirming meeting with Dr. Oates, Pat and I knew we were in the right place.

Our children thoroughly enjoyed living on the seminary campus. They became friends of Dr. and Mrs. Henlee Barnette's children, Martha and Jimmy (The Barnettes lived very close to the missionary apartment building). They explored the campus together; visited the Egyptian mummy in the seminary library and played games in the gym; swam in the indoor pool and played on the large grassy square between the administration building and the campus dormitories. As I began classes in pastoral care, Perri, Greg and Todd started classes in elementary school. Were they surprised when they saw some of their missionary friends from Brazil attending the same school (they and their parents were on furlough, too)!

Pat enjoyed making friends with professors' spouses, especially Dr. Barnette's wife, Helen. They supervised our children's activities and became good friends in the process. Pat also enjoyed discussions with me about what I was learning in pastoral care classes. She re-wrote many of my class notes (my handwriting is not good) and we enjoyed long conversations about their content and how it applied to our relationship with each other and our children.

Additionally, Crescent Hill Baptist Church was located in walking distance from the seminary campus across Grinstead Avenue. Dr. John Claypool was the pastor. We had heard about Dr. Claypool and had read some of his sermons. We joined Crescent Hill Baptist Church and were blessed by John's inspiring messages, made even more inspiring by an excellent chancel choir. We came from Brazil somewhat depleted in the inspiration department. We soon realized that we were in a church and seminary environment that would not only replenish us personally and professionally, but would re-tool us for our middle-age years ahead.

Having been the pastor of two churches and having worked with pastors in Brazil, I was able to take the element of experience to my pastoral care classes. When Dr. Swan Haworth talked about referring a counselee (when the situation is beyond your competence)—I had been there. When Dr. Oates, in his class, lectured about the tools available to a pastor or counselor, I listened with the ears of one who had been there and needed those tools in the counselor/counselee relationship. If I had taken those courses after graduating from college, I would have learned from them, I'm sure, but not like I did after having had pastoral experience. This is why I am such a strong advocate of pastors having continuing education opportunities and sabbaticals. I would like for them to say what I said often that year—"I can use that material; it will work."

What happened to Pat and me that year at Southern Seminary, however, was more than a matter of gaining new pastoral material. We experienced a personal and relational transformation. The insights we gained from my pastoral care classes were part of it. In May of 1971, following Dr. Oates' counsel, I entered a Clinical Pastoral Education program at Central State Psychiatric Hospital; this began a turning point in my life and in Pat's as well.

At Central State Hospital I was one of twelve ministers taking the program that summer. The others were: Kit Schody, Larry Roberts, George Arthur, Jack Cushman, Don Stokes, Cleve Kaiser, Roy Godwin, Ken Arentson, Phil Owens, Ron King, and Jim Leggett. Our clinical supervisors were Chaplains Clarence Barton and Franklin Duncan. Each CPE student had an assignment and functioned as a chaplain to a specific group of patients. Some of them were alcoholics. The others suffered from varying degrees of paranoia and schizophrenia. They became our spiritual flock. As chaplains in training we served with a host of other team members. Dr. Alonzo, a psychologist, was the treatment leader for M-2 where I served. Other team members were Ruth Black, head nurse; Dale Davis, social worker; Dr. Montiel, medical doctor; and Sue Southern, alcoholics' coordinator. The treatment teams met most mornings to discuss the patients care and progress. This was a growth experience for me to be a functioning member of a staff with a person-focused agenda.

Our daily activities unfolded in an orderly manner. After meeting with the treatment team, we would visit our patients—all of them—with specific attention to those who were mentioned in the team meeting for special care. There was time for reading books we would discuss in didactic seminars. There were worship seminars for presenting sermon material to be used in worship services with the patients; it was very helpful to have our sermons critiqued by fellow chaplains and supervisors. There were value-oriented seminars in which a chaplain would present a religious history of one of his patients. To care for people effectively, a minister or chaplain needs to know something about their religious background. We had clinical "clumps" to which patients were invited for conversation with a group of chaplains for therapeutic and learning purposes. Each chaplain was expected to keep a daily journal of his activities at Central State Hospital. This became a valuable tool in reflecting on one's effectiveness in ministry. The journal was used to prepare for supervisory sessions which were held periodically between a chaplain and his personal supervisor; Clarence Barton served in that role for me.

The team approach to the care of persons is an idea I embraced at Central State Hospital. One morning in the treatment team meeting Dr. Alonzo presented an idea. He said, "I would like for us to run an experiment in patient-community living. Let's work with them and let them establish their own patient government, with some genuine decision-making powers which will impact their living environment." At first, I thought—this won't work. But, Dr. Alonzo knew better than I. We shared the idea with the patients and they were, at first, hesitant and non-responsive. But as Ruth Black, the head nurse, and I kept talking to them, the patients began to warm up to the concept.

Finally, after weeks of selling the idea, we had our first patient community meeting. Ruth Black called the meeting to order. She called on me to explain again the purpose of the meeting. I shared with them Dr. Alonzo's dream about patient government and his belief that they were capable of participating in their own care and therapy. After that, they proceeded with the election of officers. Mr. Wharton Fraction was elected president.

He took charge and continued the election process. James Cessar was elected vice president and Tony Griffith was elected secretary. Ruth placed before them their first order of business. Their ward had won ten dollars for having the best poster during Alcoholism Awareness Month. She asked, "How do you want to spend it?" They decided to have a ward party. And they did! They made many other decisions during my time as their chaplain which affected their living environment. We saw chronic alcoholics, and men suffering with paranoia and schizophrenia take responsibility and participate in the improvement of their living conditions.

Learning to listen to what people say (verbally and non-verbally) and, then, responding with supportive care, was one of the lessons we learned at Central State Hospital. For example, one day while visiting patients in ward M-2, I came across four men (Gerald Cole, Lawrence Kaelin, Frank Stevens and Brovan Lee) who were chatting. They welcomed me to their conversation and Gerald shared with me a concern he was discussing with his fellow patients. He wanted to know how one could become a branch eternally related to Jesus, the Vine. We talked about the meaning of faith and the eternal nature of God's love revealed in Jesus Christ. Gerald, already a Christian, began to cry as he talked about Jesus being abandoned by the Father on the cross. In one of our didactic seminars we had discussed the meaning of tears and men's fear of being labeled weak if they cried. Gerald quickly apologized for crying and said--"Imagine me, a man, crying."

I listened to his tears for Jesus being abandoned. Behind them I heard the pain of a man, a human being, feeling alone and abandoned and, yet, feeling guilty for expressing his feelings with tears. I looked at Frank, Brovan and Lawrence; they were listening to Gerald's tears, too. I asked them, "Do you ever cry?" They said, "Yes we do." I told Gerald that I, too, cry, and that Jesus had his crying times — crying for the city of Jerusalem and at the grave of Lazarus. Gerald was relieved. He was with men who understood his masculine tears and did not judge him for shedding them.

Gerald's feelings of abandonment gave way to acceptance. We prayed together as brothers.

Some of our growth experiences at Central State Hospital came through mistakes made in the care of patients. Frank Stevens was one of the sixteen men in my care as chaplain. One day, after having had a very good conversation with Frank, I decided to invite him to a clinical clump meeting for conversation with my fellow chaplains. When I first mentioned this to Frank, he was eager to do it. I checked it out with Dr. Montiel; he gave his approval. I did not, however, mention it to Dr. Alonzo, the psychologist. Frank had received electric shock treatment for ongoing chronic, clinical depression. When I presented him in the clinical clump meeting he had just had another EST, of which I was unaware. He was disoriented and unable to have meaningful conversation with the group. The meeting ended early and I escorted Frank back to the ward. I learned, along with my colleagues, that people who suffer from acute depression are not helped by long conversations focused toward their pain. Frank had been in a cheerful mood when I invited him to the CC meeting. I should have checked with him and Dr. Alonzo before taking him to the meeting.

Writing verbatims (dialogue with patients) after counseling sessions we had with them was an essential part of the Clinical Pastoral Education process at Central State. The verbatims were written up in our daily log notebooks and evaluated by our clinical supervisors. The following is a verbatim I presented to Chaplain Clarence Barton for his evaluation (Names have been changed for confidentiality purposes).

Background: Mr. Jones is a fifty-six-year old white male. His chart has him as both deaf and mute. He is married; his wife is mute and deaf also. They have two sons, ages 14 and 18 and a daughter who is 8. The patient's family took the initiative in getting him to the hospital. Lately he had been leaving the house and getting lost. One time police were called to help find him. His memory had become faulty. John, the younger son, told Dale Davis, the social worker, that his dad started carrying a knife around the house. The family was afraid he might be thinking of suicide. They took steps to get him admitted to Central State so that he could receive help and protection.

I met John and his mother Tuesday night, July 20. They came to see Mr. Jones. We invited them to our ward party. I spoke to Mr. and Mrs. Jones through John who appears to be a well-adjusted person. He and his mother expressed concern for Mr. Jones. As they were leaving, Mrs. Jones kissed her husband, squeezed his hand and smiled. John grabbed his dad's arm and patted him on the shoulder. Mr. Jones stood looking at the door after they left. He was not able to go home but he was miserable at Central State. The next day I went to see him. We sat down and had the following conversation via paper and pencil:

Chaplain: I am Chaplain Hawkins. I'm a Baptist minister. I was glad to see your wife and son at the party last night.

Patient: (His hand shook. He paused for about a minute before writing anything). I am glad you are here.

CH: How are things going for you here at the hospital?
P: I don't know.
CH: Do you miss your wife and family?
P: Yes
CH: Do you have problems here at the hospital that you haven't been able to get across to anybody?
P: I'm guilty.
CH: I will be glad to try to help you. Is it something you would rather not tell me?
P: You are right. I want to go with you. (He is trembling all over).
CH: Where do you want us to go?
P: Help.

CH: How can I help you?

P: Help me, I'm sunk.

CH: I'm not sure I understand the word "sunk." What does it mean to you?

P: Nothing (there's a long pause).

CH: Are you worried about yourself or your family?

P: I and my family are on the same level.

CH: Do you have a telephone at home?

P: Yes – 772-3545

CH: Would you like for me to call your son and see how things are going at home?

P: Yes

CH: O.K. I'll do that and see you later today.

I called and talked with his son, John. He gave me the following information for his dad:

1. Billy Edwards, his cousin, is getting married this fall.
2. Jim, Mr. Jones' 18-year old son, is going to Army camp soon.
3. Ed and Mary, relatives, are coming down this Saturday.
4. Some of us will be out to see you either tonight or tomorrow night.
5. Mother is doing ok.

I took this news from home to Mr. Jones and left it with him. He thanked me by shaking my hand. The conversation lasted about 25 minutes. In my self-evaluation (critically important in Clinical Pastoral Education and in ministry in general) I shared with Chaplain Barton my perceived successes and mistakes. I was successful in helping Mr. Jones in his concerns about his family and being away from them. He read the news I brought him several times. I believe, at least for a while, his mind was away from the "I'm sunk" attitude and focused toward his family and their upcoming visit. I shared this information with Dale Davis so she would be in the loop as Mr. Jones' social worker. I goofed when the patient said "I'm guilty." Instead of giving him the opportunity to write about his feelings of guilt, I used a negative response which may have closed the door to possible guilt resolution. Chaplain Barton affirmed both the successes and mistakes of my interview and self-evaluation. Beside my "I goofed" comment in my verbatim write-up, he wrote — "Yeah."

All of the dimensions of the Clinical Pastoral Education program were helpful to me. The part which helped the most, though, was the Interpersonal Relations Group sessions. As we worked together as colleagues in our roles as chaplains, we also met as a group under the supervision of our clinical supervisors, Franklin Duncan and Clarence Barton. The purpose of the sessions was to listen to ourselves (self-awareness) as we listened to what our colleagues shared in the sessions. In other words: Can we really hear what others are saying — patients, counselees, parishioners, family members, etc. — if we are not aware of the conversation going on within ourselves at the same time? These internal factors can be "blind spots" where past experiences are kept from our present awareness and, yet, still impact our behavior and relationships unconsciously. They can cause us to be fearful, judgmental, hostile, distant, etc. If we do not learn to be self-aware as we listen to and communicate with others, we may wind up projecting our "blind spots" on them and miss what they are actually saying. So, in our IPR groups we listened inwardly and outwardly under the supervision of two men who had been certified to guide us through the CPE and IPR disciplines.

The goal of our therapy sessions was, as Jesus said it: "…to be wise as serpents and harmless as doves" (Matthew 10:16), as persons and ministers. There were times when our sharing took the form of comfort and affirmation; at other times, however, there was anger and confrontation. For example, one day we listened to Roy Simms as he shared about a painful experience in his recent past. (I am using different names). He had been asked to resign by the members of the church he was serving as a student pastor. He and his wife were hurt and they left the church with unresolved feelings of hostility and guilt. We listened to Roy and various group members who gave him positive strokes of comfort and support. Roy received the affirmation well but still wrestled with the question — why was I unable to lead the church through conflict to a positive relational outcome?

That's where Roy had a blind spot in his self-image. At times in our group activities he projected an image of someone who was in total control of himself and his emotions — stiff and superior. When he was confronted with this observation by Bob Little, his face turned red and he became defensive. Then Bob identified with Roy. He shared with him and our group that he, too, was wrestling with the I-want-to-control-everything attitude and was beginning to understand a past impacting factor; he said his mother was the type person who wanted to have everything just so-so. Bob, an only child, had identified with his mother, becoming like her and resenting it at the same time. Roy began to see a similar pattern between himself and his father who was a strong, controlling person. Our group, for a while, became a battlefield between Roy and Bob — one from a patriarchal family and one from a matriarchal family. We saw, however, self-awareness begin to reshape two colleagues into more accessible, caring human beings. The past parental influences were still there but they were no longer blind spots. They had become allies in the light and not enemies in their ongoing relationships as persons and ministers.

At first, in our IPR sessions, I listened but said very little. My basic feeling was one of fear. I heard Roy and Bob (and others) sharing their feelings. I knew that my deeper feelings were being held inside, guarded by a sentinel with an invisible sign which said, "No trespassing." I had been a good husband, father, pastor and missionary. But, something was missing. I saw that missing part in Chaplain Clarence Barton. As he supervised and participated in our IPR sessions, I observed in him a man who was both competent and spontaneous. He was humorous and thoughtful. As I listened and observed him, I asked myself — "where is your spontaneity?" I had been spontaneous as a child. But that child with his freedom to be, had been locked up inside of me. Childhood illness was a factor. But my mother's painful journey through menopause was the major trauma which impacted my emotional life as a child. In response to her pain and, at times, erratic and unpredictable emotional behavior, I developed a mistrust of expressions of emotion. Keeping emotions under control, in my young and fearful mind was the secure way to be and live.

I found in my dad a model to follow. After losing both parents and his only sibling, a brother, when he was in middle childhood, he had learned to hunker down and endure times of emotional stress. I over-identified with him and resisted my mother's spontaneity of feelings as being somehow dangerous. All of this was a matter of looking back and becoming aware of how my past was still alive in my life as a grown man. Don't get me wrong — my parents were good people who had come through tough times. And they, also, had parents who gave them both care and challenges.

I shared my story with the group. There was affirmation and understanding. Clarence Barton and I made a contract to work on my need to trust my emotions and release my inner child to play and work more spontaneously. My self-disclosure turned out to be a turning point in my life, both personally and professionally.

Along with the impact of the IPR sessions on my self-awareness and emotional maturing, I want to mention two other contributing factors. One came from our years in Brazil. Brazilian men greeted one another with an "abraco", which we call a "bear hug." Men in my family didn't do that. When we returned from Brazil, I put my arms around Dad and he pulled away. To him, that was not a sign of masculine affection. I didn't give up, however. Eventually, after some awkwardness, Dad, my brothers and I started greeting each other with bear hugs. We went to Brazil to be missionaries; they became missionaries to us in how to express affection more openly.

The other factor which helped me was my exposure to transactional analysis. Eric Berne made this method of learning the dynamics of emotional behavior popular in his book, <u>Games People Play</u>. (Grove Press, Inc. New York, 1964) Dr. Berne put into simple language some of the more complex theories about human nature and how we handle relationships. Simply stated, he says all of us have three internal states or dimensions, impacted by childhood and adolescent influences (parents, family, teachers, ministers, etc.) from which we communicate with others.

The first dimension is our internal parent. It is the control and conscience part of who we are. Parents do this for their children while they are small. But through childhood and adolescence, one of the purposes of parenting is to instill in children their own internal parent, capable of guiding them into and through their adult lives. If the instilled parent is a healthy one, the maturing process will unfold and produce a mature adult. The instilling process, however, is never done to perfection. The stories from the Bible and history in general are testimonies to that fact. All of our emerging internal parents will need continuing, redeeming alterations and improvements. Perfection is just not possible.

The second dimension from which we communicate with others is our internal child. The child is where we feel, cry, play, and express sexual, hostile and spontaneous emotions. The purpose of our internal parent is not to squelch the internal child but to guide it to a healthy and happy blending of responsibility and freedom of expression in adult relationships. This, I think, was one of the things Jesus wanted Nicodemus and his colleagues to see when He talked about being born again (John 3:1-21). Nicodemus and his fellow religionists had internalized strong, demanding parents which had imprisoned their internal child. Jesus saw them as grown men who needed to rediscover their childlikeness.

The third state from which we communicate is the internal adult. The adult is the internal blender which mixes the messages from the parent and child and passes them on to others—spouses, children, grandchildren, colleagues, counselees, etc. If the internal parent is too strong, too brittle or too demanding, the message to the receiver will be condescending (or, "I'm the parent and you are the child"). If the internal child is dominant over a weak internal parent, the message sent may be emotionally irresponsible for lack of a mature internal parent.

Dr. Berne contends that all of us have our internal states—parent, adult, child—from which we communicate with others. He further contends that we tend to play games by unconsciously imposing old scripts from our past on current relationships. These games can show up in family relationships and in the business world among peers.

As I was finishing my role as chaplain at Central State Hospital, Pat and I began to identify relational games we were playing as parents and spouses. In relating to our children, Pat was the parent; I was the child. Our relationship was, therefore, over/under and conflicted. She was more controlling and I was more permissive. Our children, of course, learned how to "work" that arrangement. When it came to finances and money, however, I was the parent; Pat was the child.

Looking honestly and critically at our relationship, though, we began to realize we were playing games—and the games were not for fun but control. Why were we that way? We began to poke around in our past, and there it was. Pat grew up under the influence of a very strict grandmother, which, in turn, helped to construct in her a strong internal parent. She loved our children dearly but was super vigilant in her maternal care. On the other hand, I grew up with lots of freedom to explore nature away from home. Pat wanted to keep a tight grip on our children; I wanted them to have more freedom.

Money was another matter. In that area, family finances, where I was the parent and she was the child, our past was determinative. My parents were good people but poor managers of money. I heard lots of arguments between Mom and Dad about money issues. As a child and adolescent I made a vow to myself (we do make such vows about our future)—when I grow up and marry, we'll be more careful about our money. It was not a written vow—most likely not a conscious one. Pat, on the other hand, grew up in a family where finances were never discussed openly. Her parents were not wealthy. Her dad owned a small furniture store and her mother worked as a hairdresser, owning her own business; money was provided but not argued over. After Pat and I got married, our past lived on in our relationship. We began to observe, however, the over/under games we were playing with each other and with our children. As we did, we were able, through self-awareness, to call the games off.

The old scripts we bring with us out of childhood and adolescence don't vanish. They are still there. Pat still has some of her grandmother in her and I still am conservative about money (Living on a minister's salary, we had to be somewhat conservative). But Pat and I were able to see the games and understand their sources and rebalance the way we related as husband and wife and as parents. As I became less conservative with money, she became more responsible. We were doing those good things together with intentionality. As I became more responsible with our children, Pat was able to free up her internal child and become more playful with them.

Let me illustrate: One day, shortly after finishing CPE training at Central State Hospital, we had a family Pow-Wow. We were sitting on the floor in our missionary apartment. As we shared, Perri said something like this, "Mom, you don't get down and play with us when we're playing games." Previously, Pat would have by-passed the invitation to let her internal child come out and play with our children. But, suddenly Pat did a beautiful and different thing. She reached over and grabbed Perri around the neck and pulled her down. The two of them rolled over on the floor, laughing like two giddy children at play. The boys and I stared in surprise and then joined in the spontaneous fun. Pat and I were still the parents. We were learning, though, to be more resident in the present with each other and our children and less impacted by some of the negatives of our past. Our future was looking brighter.

Choosing a topic for my Master of Theology degree thesis was my next big challenge at Southern Baptist Theological Seminary. I asked Dr. John Boyle, a professor in the Department of Pastoral Care, to be my thesis supervisor. He agreed and helped me to choose a thesis related to practical ministry where I would have a role as both minister and researcher. That role was chaplain at the Children's Diagnostic Center, an affiliate of the Louisville University Medical School. Dr. Wayne E. Oates, along with being Senior Professor of Psychology of Religion at Southern Seminary, was also serving as Professor of Psychiatry and Behavioral Sciences at the Medical School. His dynamic leadership opened many doors for students to become ministers and researchers in the Louisville Multiversity community.

As chaplain at the diagnostic center, I served with the diagnostic team and provided spiritual counseling for parents of children with mental health issues. They brought their children to the center for evaluation but needed spiritual care and encouragement as well. As I listened to their concerns for their children, I began to hear a recurring theme — feelings of guilt about having had a mentally handicapped child. Most often the guilt feelings were religious in nature. Some of them felt that God was punishing them for past sins — related to sex or church attendance, etc. They expressed a particular kind of grief, but at times tried to hide it from themselves. The birth of a child is supposed to be a happy time. They had experienced, however, the death of the expected child which cannot be ritualized through a grief process and the birth of the real child who deserves celebration and acceptance. So, the parents tended to hide their grief all alone and celebrate the real child with feelings of guilt and questions of — "why us?" My role as chaplain was to listen and share with them a message of hope, understanding, and forgiveness.

One young couple shared with me all of their positive feelings about having had a Down syndrome boy. That was ok; they were being honest — those feelings were there and were genuine. But they were tense. I said to them, "Thank you for sharing with me your positive feelings about your son. I'm sure you will give him all the love he will need to grow, and be a happy and productive person. If, however, you have other feelings, I believe those are ok and I believe God accepts and understands those feelings, too." When I said that, the whole conversation changed. They relaxed and began to share with me their grief and hurt. They trusted me with their joy and sorrow. And that gave me an opportunity to share with them a message of hope and forgiveness.

Hope came in the form of an invitation to join a group composed of parents who also had Down syndrome children; there were several such groups springing up in the Louisville area. They welcomed the opportunity to be in a support group. The forgiveness came not for a confession on their part of some secret sin for which they were being punished. It came from understanding the incomplete nature of the creation to which all of us belong. The apostle Paul alludes to this incompleteness in the book of Romans (Romans 8:18-23): "We know that the whole creation has been groaning in travail together until now; and not only the creation, but we ourselves, who have the first fruits of the Spirit, groan inwardly as we wait for adoption as sons, the redemption of our bodies." Paul sees the whole creation, including us, waiting for wholeness. In this world, however, all of us participate in the creation's incompleteness.

Hope and forgiveness come when we accept our incompleteness, and that of others, including a Down syndrome son, not as punishment but as part of a good creation moving toward fulfillment and redemption. The young couple I counseled that day, and the other approximately twenty couples I counseled at the diagnostic center, left their evaluation experiences feeling freer and more hopeful about their parenting and children's futures. My counseling sessions with the parents, plus researching books and articles on guilt, forgiveness, hope and mental illness, became the bases of my Master of Theology Degree thesis "Forgiveness As a Factor in the Management of Guilt in Parents of Mentally Retarded Children."

Before finishing the requirements to receive my degree, Pat and I realized it would take longer than our year of furlough. So, I wrote to the Foreign Mission Board and requested a six month extension to complete my academic work. The extension was approved. Then, in one of those times of self-evaluation, Pat and I began to assess our future, and that of our children, in light of our roles as missionaries and our growth experiences at Southern Seminary. I shared with Pat that after serving as chaplain at Central State Hospital and the diagnostic center, I realized I was a pastor at heart, not a teacher. Pat looked at me and said, "I've been having some of those same thoughts and can't see us going back to Brazil." After talking it over with our children and praying, we made a decision to share our decision with the Foreign Mission Board.

I wrote a letter of resignation in which I presented my belief that a Brazilian pastor, competent in the Portuguese language, trained in principles and skills of pastoral care, would be a better teacher for Brazilian Baptist theological students. I guess we could have waited until the end of the six months extension to share our decision; that would not have been honest, however. It was, of course, risky to relinquish our missionary salary. But Pat and I were convinced it was the right decision for us and our children.

The Foreign Mission Board shared our decision with our colleagues in Brazil. They and the Board requested that we reconsider. We appreciated that gesture of confidence but, having a sense of peace in our hearts, we shared with Brazil and the Board that our decision was final.

I told Dr. John Boyle, my thesis supervisor, about our decision. He picked up the phone and called Dr. Walter Jackson, a colleague of his at Southern Seminary and a member of Melbourne Heights Baptist Church. That same day I received a call from the chairman of the church's Pastor Search Committee; the church needed a pastor and I needed a church.

I became the pastor of Melbourne Heights Baptist Church in the winter of 1972. The church, located at 3728 Taylorsville Road, Louisville, Kentucky, originated as a mission of Louisville's Walnut Street Baptist Church before becoming a constituted church in 1957. Located in the Hikes Point area of Jefferson County, a suburban community of Louisville, the church had approximately 600 members when I became the pastor. Reverend Bill Rogers was my immediate predecessor. Bill and his family remained in the church as he assumed a staff position with the Kentucky Baptist Convention in the area of race relations. Bill and I, at his initiative, entered an unwritten covenant to make our co-existence in the church a positive for its ministry.

The death of one of our members, just days into my leadership at Melbourne Heights, put the covenant to work. The deceased man's wife reached out to Bill as the pastor she knew (In grief we naturally are comforted more by the familiar). When she called, Bill agreed to help but suggested that I be invited to the first home visit for comfort and funeral planning. Bill and I went as colleagues to her home and gave her support. Then, in the funeral service, we gave the kind of co-leadership which sought to demonstrate that we were servants of the church and its servant leader, Jesus Christ. Bill helped to pave the way for me to have a soft landing as new pastor. Our colleague covenant would continue to work.

After purchasing our first house in east Louisville on Hanover Drive, our children were delighted with more bedroom space. And, in no time, they transformed our full basement into a game room for the neighborhood kids and the youth of our church. While Pat was busy decorating our house, I was busy adjusting to our new church family. As I sought divine leadership and met with the church's leadership, a theme began to emerge. In our first church the theme was reconciliation. In the second it was grief support. At Melbourne Heights it would be experimentation.

During the sixties and into the seventies there had been a mood of experimentation and change in the country. That mood, no doubt, had challenged seminaries and churches to examine established structures and methods and to try new ways to express and implement the enduring truths of the Christian faith. After my recent experiences as a graduate student at Southern Seminary, including serving as a leader of one of Dr. Oates' Pastoral Psychology class sub-groups (dealing with church rituals), I was ready to lead the church as a change agent. Bill Rogers had led the church to be open to that kind of pastoral leadership. And our church, fortunately, had ready access to speakers from the seminary community. They spoke at various times, inspiring and challenging the church to be a context for innovative ministry. Some of the professors who blessed Melbourne Heights Church during the 70's were: Dr. Wayne Oates, Dr. John Boyle, Dr. Swan Hayworth, Dr. D.L. Moody, Dr. Ann Davis, Dr. Phil Landgrave, Dr. Bill Leonard, Dr. Walter Jackson, Dr. William Hull, Dr. Findley Edge, Dr. Frank Stagg and Dr. Daniel Bagby.

It seemed almost inevitable that our church as a context for ministry experimentation would be impacted by its seminary connections. And, indeed, it was. In the summer of 1972, Dr. John Boyle asked me to serve as a supervisor for students taking PR 151, the basic course in pastoral care. It was understood that the setting for the supervisory experience would be the Melbourne Heights Baptist Church field. After obtaining approval and support from the church, the program was begun. For two semesters, fall 1972 and spring 1973, the program consisted of four dimensions of pastoral training.

First, the students obtained theological and theoretical training in the classroom. Second, under my supervision, they accepted a particular area in which they were to function as pastoral interns. They were: ministry to the elderly, hospital ministry, ministry to single adults, crisis ministry, youth ministry and ministry to children. Third, once a week I met with the interns. At times we analyzed verbatims the students submitted from the various areas for which they were responsible. Quite often this led to collective decision-making concerning specific needs in church members' lives. Fourth, each student had individual access to me in communicating problems and needs encountered in ministry. The intern program did not negate the involvement of the church's lay people in ministry. Each intern served with a deacon shepherd (the church's diaconate had transitioned to a service model and no longer functioned as an administrative board).

During the summer of 1973 Dr. Oates contacted me in order to reflect on the program's effectiveness and project toward future possibilities. He communicated his sense of satisfaction concerning the results he had observed in the participating students. They described to him their pastoral care experience in a local church setting as being both comprehensive and practical. I shared with Dr. Oates the positive feedback I had received from persons to whom the interns had ministered. From dialogue and discussions, both in the Department of Psychology of Religion at Southern Seminary, and among our church leadership, a decision was made to intensify the church's role in the program. Oates suggested that a pilot project be attempted in the church. This would be an experiment in preparation for clinical pastoral education with the local church as its instructional context. The pilot project began in September, 1973. Dr. Daniel Bagby, instructor in Psychology of Religion at Southern Seminary served as the academic supervisor; I was the pastoral supervisor.

Classes in the church fellowship hall were held on Monday afternoons from two to four-thirty during the fall semester. Along with accepting specific pastoral assignments, each student served with a deacon in caring for approximately ten families. Dr. Bagby and I gave close supervision to the interns who met in a group once a week. On the basis of the pilot project's apparent effectiveness two decisions were made. First, the project would continue during the spring semester of that year. Second, a Clinical Pastoral Education program would be attempted at Melbourne Heights Baptist Church in the near future.

The "near future" happened in September, 1974. Our church decided to be the context for an experimental Clinical Pastoral Education program in a church field setting. That coincided with my decision, with the church's approval, to enter the Doctor of Ministry Degree program at Southern Seminary. My doctoral thesis (project paper) would be: The Development of a Clinical Pastoral Education Program as an Aid to Ministry at Melbourne Heights Baptist Church. The church was not certified as a CPE institution. The participating students understood that. They were willing, however, to receive CPE in a local church setting as an experiment beyond its usual hospital environment.

The students, four of them, were more than pastoral interns. The church (with a small ministerial staff) agreed to give the students ministerial staff status. The interns had felt that their status had been somewhat peripheral. The CPE students had a ministerial title: Jack Maguire was Minister of Education; Sue Sparks was Minister to Senior Adults; Ann Stafford was Minister to Children; Joe Brown was minister to Youth. The CPE program at Melbourne Heights Church proved to be quite a blessing. The church grew numerically and in its outreach to the larger community. The students in their evaluations were very positive about their growth in becoming more effective as ministers. The church was very affirming of the program in its evaluation. My Doctor of Ministry thesis was approved and I received my Doctor of Ministry degree. And Dr. Oates, the visionary who dreamed of CPE in a local church setting, assessed the Melbourne Heights experiment as a possible door-opener to his dream's further implementation.

Frank, graduation day, Doctor of Ministry, at Southern Baptist Theological Seminary, Louisville, KY, May 1975

Before we leave the CPE theme, I want to share with you a conversation I had with Dr. Oates in the hall outside his seminary office. Its content had nothing to do with the Clinical Pastoral Education program. Dr. Oates said, "Frank, I have a concern about our son, Bill. He served in Viet Nam and is home now. Could you drop by and see him and see if some of your singles might reach out to him? He lives alone and just can't seem to get going again. I would appreciate your help." I promised my mentor that I would do everything I could to reach Bill. And I did. I visited him in his home. Some of our singles went to see him. Bill was cordial but not responsive to our attempts to become new friends. It pained me to share that kind of news with Dr. Oates who was to me a spiritual giant. Heartaches come to us all, even those we respect with admiration and awe.

Please do not think that seminary student involvement was the only area of experimentation at Melbourne Heights Church. One day one of our ladies came to me after we had celebrated communion. She said, "Pastor, is there anything we can do to make communion more meaningful? We do it the same way every time and it seems so dull. It's too important to be that way." I was irritated for a while. Then I thought—she might be right. I talked it over with our staff and we decided to have our next communion service at night in the fellowship hall. That was entirely new for the church and me.

We put candles on the tables and placed the elements at the head of each table where a deacon would sit and serve family-style. The youth choir sang some of their inspirational music and I did a brief devotional entitled, "Come to the Table." All of us have tables to which we have been invited—in our childhood and youth—and tables to which we have invited others—our children, family and friends. Jesus continues the family motif by inviting us to the table he prepares with his own blood and body. After the devotional and prayer, with soft background music, the deacons began the table communion conversation as the elements were shared from person to person around the tables. The fellowship hall was transformed into sanctuary. For the first time in my life one of my children shared with me the bread and the cup. I had never shared this sacred meal to Pat individually. That night, however, as members were talking around the tables like families do, I served

Pat and said, "Pat, I am honored to share with you this bread and juice as our Lord commanded us to do; I love you."

As we communed at the tables, we heard someone crying We thought—these must be tears of joy. When the service was over, we found out what happened. The tears came from one of our young single women.

A little history: About a year prior to that evening she was driving to a wedding rehearsal; her mother was with her. Paula lost control of the car and there was a tragic accident. She was hospitalized for weeks with multiple injuries. Her mother died. Paula was so traumatized by the tragedy that her conscious mind could not grieve or admit what had happened. She had remained in a state of unresolved grief until that night. The Lord's Table became Paula's safe place to own and share her grief. She began to talk about her mother, and as the pent up tears flowed, the healing which she needed was mediated through communion and friends gathered around her at the table.

While we were with Melbourne Heights Church, I had many opportunities to serve as pastor/counselor to our church members. One Wednesday evening a young husband stopped me after a Royal Ambassador meeting (he was an R.A. leader). He said, "Frank, do you have a minute?" I responded, "Sure, David." He said, "Frank, I've got a problem at work" (I thought it was probably work-related). But he continued—"It's not the job—it's a woman. She's offering herself to me. And, I don't know how to handle it." I said, "You mean she wants to go to bed with you?" "Yes, she comes to me during break-time and turns on the charm." "Have you done anything wrong with her"? "No, but I don't know what to say to her; I don't want to make a scene." "David, have you shared this with your wife"? David's eyes got big. "No, no I haven't." "Is there any reason why you can't"? "I guess not." "David, why don't you share it with Peggy? Then the two of you can decide how you will respond to the woman." David reluctantly agreed to tell Peggy. That Friday I received a phone call from David. He said, "Frank, it worked!" I said, "What happened?" "I told Peggy and she was upset. But when she settled down we made a decision about what I would say to the woman. Sure enough — at break-time that day — she sat down where I was sitting and started again. Frank, I looked at her and said, 'I want you to know I told my wife about you and she and I have decided there's no room in our relationship for you.' " "What did she do, David"? "She grabbed her lunch and moved to another table." "And what did Peggy say when you told her"? "She hugged me, kissed me and said, 'Honey, do you know how much I love you?'" Evil retreats in the presence of that kind of honesty, integrity and love.

"Pastor, I need to talk to you; can we meet for dinner tonight?" I noted a sense of urgency in Reggie's voice. "What time do you have in mind, Reggie"? "I can pick you up at your home at 6 o'clock; is that ok?" "Yes, I'll be ready." Reggie was one of the lay leaders in our church. He served in a role which gave him decision-making power which affected the church budget, and just about every aspect of our church's ministry. He was very conservative and thought the church should be that way, too. There were clashes between Reggie and other lay leaders. At the church staff level, there was an attempt to keep Reggie's overbearing attitude from affecting the church's growth. This was difficult, however, given Reggie's tendency to talk down to lay peers and church staff personnel as well.

What did Reggie want to talk to me about over dinner? I was puzzled. We traveled some miles from Louisville to one of Colonial Sander's special restaurants. As we were eating, Reggie opened up and shared with me about a crisis he was facing at work. He had a responsible job in a reputable company. The day before, his supervisor called him to his office and gave him an ultimatum — "Either you shape up or you're out of here." "Shaping up" had to do with Reggie's relationship with other company staff members who were Reggie's peers. They had finally told their supervisor —

it's either Reggie or us—we can no longer tolerate him treating us like he's our boss. Reggie had tears in his eyes as he told me his boss was giving him six weeks to shape up or be terminated. He looked at me across the table and said, "Frank, what do I need to do? I need my job."

In that moment I saw a man who had reached a critical point in his life and career. What had been happening at church was also happening at his workplace. His talking down to people was a pattern. I wanted to be supportive to Reggie but I knew he needed more from me than a pastoral affirmation, prayer and "it will get better, Reggie." So, I ventured a question—"Reggie, how do you think your co-workers see you relating to them?" He hesitated for several seconds and then answered, "I guess they see me as an "a-hole" who tries to boss them around. Look, Frank, I am conservative and want things to be done right. I'm beginning to see I probably take it too far." He paused. Then he asked, "Do I come across like that at church?"

Reggie had reached a teachable moment of self-awareness. He did not need, and, I was confident he did not want easy reassurance that would temporarily take him away from his pain. He needed to make some serious changes or lose his job. I said, "Reggie, you've asked an honest question and I'm going to give you an honest answer. Yes, that's the way you relate at church, too." Then I added, "But Reggie, the redeeming thing about our conversation tonight is this—you are asking the questions about yourself. I know it must be painful and I want to be your pastor and friend. But you have to decide how you will respond to your pain." He looked at me and said, "Frank, do you remember the old song—'It's me, it's me, it's me O Lord, standin' in the need of prayer—well, it's me. I need to change. I'll always be conservative, but I've got to change or I'll lose my job."

Reggie did change! He kept his job. And, at church, people were asking, "What has happened to Reggie?" He was still conservative but he mellowed out and became a team player. Some would call it behavior modification. In church language we call it—repentance; that's when the doors to God's Kingdom are open to us for redemptive life-changes. Jesus proclaimed this good news at the beginning of his earthly ministry—"Repent, for the Kingdom of heaven is at hand" (Matthew 4:17).

One snowy evening in February, 1973 I visited in the home of Jim and Bonnie Kirkpatrick. They had four children—Jim's two (a boy and a girl) and Bonnie's two (a boy and a girl). Bonnie had called and said the children wanted to talk to me about becoming Christians and being baptized. That kind of home visit ranks at the top of pastoral joy-producers. I talked to them with positive results; they chose to be baptized the following Sunday. Then, I looked at Jim. He had been listening carefully to our conversation. I said, "Jim, this would be a wonderful opportunity for you to lead your children in Christian baptism." Without any hesitation he said, "I'm ready; I want to be a Christian father." The following Sunday evening I baptized Jim first and then the children. A dad had assumed the role of parental leadership in one of life's most important decisions—following Christ in Christian baptism.

Pat and I became good friends with the Kirkpatricks and, to our pleasant surprise, were invited by them to attend the Kentucky Derby that May. Jim worked in Colonel Sander's Kentucky Fried Chicken Headquarters and had four tickets for that year's big event. Our box seats were above and a little to the left of the finish line. We witnessed the gala fanfare of the Churchill Down's phenomena—the incredible hats, the infield activities, the races before the "big race", and then, "My Old Kentucky Home."

Pat and I did not bet on any of the races but chose winners, to have fun. She chose about 4 winners in a row. Some of the men, in nearby boxes, began, with mint julips in hand, to observe her choices. Then it happened in the big race—we saw that incredible horse—Secretariat—zoom across the finish line and make racehorse history. We had been in the right place at the right time as a byproduct gift from doing ministry in Jesus' name. The greatest gift, however, did not happen at Churchill Downs but in our church baptistry.

Bill Rogers led Melbourne Heights Baptist Church to be involved in building healthy race relations before I became the church's pastor. For example, he developed a close friendship with Rev. Thurmond Coleman, the pastor of a nearby African American Baptist Church. From that friendship the two churches became friends and initiated joint worship services and fellowship meals prepared by church members. I, too, became a friend of Rev. Coleman, and, together, we continued to lead our churches to worship and eat together. Thurmond was an excellent preacher and had another gift I did not have—a beautiful singing voice. In one of our joint worship services (in our church's sanctuary), their choir sang and Rev. Coleman stood up to preach but remembered a song he loved to hear his choir sing. So, he said, "Choir, sing again before I preach" (song's title I don't remember). They sang it beautifully and with great fervor to the delight of our congregation. While they sang, I thought, I would never attempt that with Barry Combs, our Minister of Music, and the Chancel Choir. We were blessed by their spontaneity and Brother Thurmond's inspiring message which he ended with a song as he sat down. Some of our members suggested that I end some sermons that way. They were, of course, kidding, and they knew it and so did I. I was myself when we worshipped with Rev. Thurmond and his church family. They accepted my preaching and our choirs singing and affirmed both as different but inspiring in their own unique way.

Thurmond and I had the kind of friendship which led to occasions of mutual support. I remember a day when we were drinking coffee together. He had called and wanted to talk to me. We met at a restaurant and I could tell he was carrying a burden. He said, "Frank, I've got a situation and don't know how to handle it." I listened as a father shared from his heart about his son. The son had joined the United States Air Force and was stationed in Germany. Very soon he would be home on furlough. I thought— why should that be hard to handle. Then Thurmond shared with me that his son had met a young lady and was bringing her home. Again, I thought—so, that happens often. Thurmond then looked at me with pain on his face and said, "Frank, she's a blonde-haired white girl and my church family won't accept her. I couldn't help but think of the movie, "Guess Who's Coming for Dinner?"

I don't think Thurmond thought I had any magical answers to his dilemma. He just needed to share his burden with a friend. He knew, as well as I, some of the painful complexities of race relations. And, in that vein, told me about a young white couple which joined their church but left after several months; the children of his church would not accept the couple's white children. Thurmond was being confessional about prejudice in his own congregation. He knew he could trust me with that data as a Christian brother and that I would support him and his family. I pledged to do that through prayer. Being a minister colleague I wanted to do more. I said, "Thurmond, if they plan to get married and you need help—I'll assist you or officiate at the ceremony." Thurmond's face showed emotion and he said, "Thanks Frank, I appreciate that." Thurmond never called on me to help with a wedding. That meeting at the restaurant, however, had taken our friendship to a deeper and more realistic level.

MIDDLE AGE — BECOMING A MATURE ME

It's full summer — time to produce

In our fourth year at Melbourne Heights Baptist Church I celebrated my 40th birthday. Young adulthood was ending. Middle age was beginning for Pat and me (she was ten months younger than I). We were finishing what Louis J. Sherrill calls the stage of choosing life's basic identifications. We had chosen each other as life partners in marriage. And, together, we had chosen a ministerial career for our life's work. We had sought to become established in our chosen profession. That had involved serving three churches, five years of missionary service in Brazil and additional academic work at Southern Seminary.

The time for choosing and becoming established, though, was ending. Middle age was upon us — the time for full maturity and maximum responsibility. Paul Tournier sees middle age in seasonal terms as mid-summer (Paul Tournier, <u>The Seasons of Life</u>: John Knox Press, Atlanta, Georgia, 1974). It's that time of life when becoming established usually gives way to maintenance (According to Donald Super — already referenced). We are in our vocational place and maintain ourselves there into retirement. And just as green is the dominant color of summer, we need "green" to support our offspring through academia and weddings into their (hopefully) independent status. Just as summer is at its greatest peak in terms of productivity, our output is challenged to maximize its potentials. If we do not reach reasonable maturity in our summer years, chances are we will go kicking and screaming into old age.

Developmental maturity tends to orient itself in two directions. First, there is gratitude toward our past. Immaturity seems to color the past with black strokes; maturity sees the past — parents, families and self — in terms of blessings and imperfections.

Both are accepted in the present in the ongoing drama of creative living in an imperfect world. Erik Erikson says one of the signs of this kind of maturity is the ability to accept one's past as being non-negotiable; we can't trade it off. When we can accept it, with its flaws and virtues, we are ready to move on as grateful selves toward achieving a greater maturity.

Pat and I were entering our middle-age years. We had followed the growth angel through childhood, adolescence and young adulthood. The ubiquitous summons was being heard again in our bodies, minds and souls—"This way please."

The telephone rang in my church office. Ruth Jones, our church secretary said, "Frank, Dr. Henlee Barnette wants to speak with you." I wondered—"What does the head of the seminary's Ethics Department want to speak with me about?" I'll never forget what he said when I answered—"Frank, what heresy are you up to at Melbourne Heights Church?" I said, "Well, it depends on what the needs are, Dr. Barnette." He laughed and said, "Well, don't be surprised if some strange-looking people show up at your church one of these Sundays. Now, don't get out your sugar stick, Frank; just be your ole' mean self." That was "Barnette-speak" for—you may have a Pastor Search committee visit very soon. Dr. Barnette was right.

On Mother's Day, 1975 two members of the First Baptist Church of Statesboro, Georgia worshipped in our sanctuary. About two weeks later, I received a call from the chairman of the committee, inviting Pat and me to visit Statesboro and to have conversation with the full committee. I told Dr. Robertson that we would pray about it and call him back. Pat and I knew this was major decision-making time for us. This was true for several reasons. Dr. Swan Hayworth, one of my mentors in the Department of Pastoral Care, had left Southern Seminary to become the Director of Pastoral Care at Bowman Grey Baptist Hospital in Winston-Salem, North Carolina. He had recently contacted me to see if I might be interested in being the hospital chaplain. He said the compensation package was low but there would be interim pastor opportunities in the Winston-Salem area. A part of me wanted to say yes to Dr. Hayworth's offer. Then, at the same time, Dr. Ed Thornton was becoming the new Senior Professor of Psychology of Religion at Southern Seminary due to Dr. Wayne Oates' retirement. Dr. Thornton was interested in continuing Dr. Oates' initiative in exploring Clinical Pastoral Education in the local church as a viable extension to the hospital setting. He knew we had done that at Melbourne Heights and wanted to discuss with me the possibility of advancing the concept beyond the experimental state.

Pat and I prayerfully considered our options and decided that our gifts were better suited for pastoral ministry in a local church setting. We would always be grateful for our five years in Louisville, Kentucky. What we experienced at Central State Hospital, the seminary campus, and at Melbourne Heights Church, changed our lives and prepared us for pastoral ministry through middle age toward retirement.

One of the pleasant surprises Pat and I had when we met with the Pastor Search Committee in Statesboro, GA, was Dr. Pope Duncan. He had been one of my professors at Southeastern Baptist Theological Seminary in the late fifties. Dr. Duncan had become president of Georgia Southern College (now — Georgia Southern University). He was serving as both deacon and Pastor Search Committee member. We then knew how our name was placed with the PSC. Henlee Barnette and Pope were friends. That solved the puzzle of why Dr. Barnette called me about an upcoming visit. Our visit to Statesboro went well and after another visit to the church and the traditional "trial sermon," I received and accepted the call to be the pastor of the First Baptist Church of Statesboro, Georgia. I told Dr. Duncan that just as he had graded my papers in seminary, I was going to grade him as a deacon. He didn't seem threatened at all.

When we left Louisville, our family experienced acute grief. We had grieved when we had left other places, also. But Louisville had been the place where our children had become teenagers. Perri and Greg had had their first dates there. Todd had reached age twelve and was on the verge of the teenage explosion. Their grief in leaving sweethearts and peer groups intensified the grief which Pat and I felt in leaving a place and a people to which we had become emotionally attached. Our experience was not unique, however. We were experiencing what countless persons encounter in our highly mobile society. One statement, though, which Perri made in the midst of her transitional grief proved to be prophetic. She said to Pat one day while we were attempting to sell our house (it sold during our last week in Louisville), "Mom, I wouldn't mind moving to Statesboro if you were pregnant." Perri's comment provided us a moment of laughter which gave relief to our pain in leaving.

We moved into the church's parsonage in August, 1975, just in time for our children to start classes in their new schools. The teenagers in our church were very helpful in making that transition go smoothly for Perri, Greg and Todd. New friendships developed to make less painful their lost ones. Pat was thrilled with the music program of our new church. Dr. Warren Fields was the Minister of Music (as well as a professor in the music department of Georgia Southern). His wife, Bobbie, who was also an accomplished musician, became one of our closest friends. Pat joined the Chancel Choir and gained new friends, especially Babs Jordan, a contemporary of mine at Furman University and the wife of Dr. James Jordan, also a Furman grad, and head of the History Department at GS and Billie Lane, church organist (with whom she played many piano/organ programs.) Dr. Warren Fields, fortunately, was just one member of an excellent ministerial staff at the church. The other members were: Rev. Stan Hill, Associate Minister of Education and Administration and Rev. Tom Byerly, Associate Pastor and Minister to Youth. The church also had an outstanding support staff: three secretaries, a church dietician, church custodian and two maids. Under the leadership of Dr. J. Robert Smith, my predecessor, the church had grown significantly. When he retired in December, 1974 the church had about two thousand members, for whom four ministers were appropriate and needed.

I was ready to supervise the ministerial staff and they responded well to my style of leadership. From my recent academic training in pastoral care, I had grown to see the good news of Christianity in "both/and" terms. It was for both individuals and relationships. My preaching and ministerial staff leadership followed that motif. Along with addressing administrative and program-focused issues in staff meetings, we began to look at our church as people and ask, "How can we make the message of Christ relevant for people in the relationships where they live every day?"

Our staff meetings came alive — we began talking about real people and real relationships and how we could design ministry to make the gospel message impactful for them (spouses, parents, children, friends, co-workers, etc.). Confidentiality was guarded as a sacred trust, but relationships became a mission field addressed in the pulpit and in our staff meetings. Tom, Stan and Warren responded well to that approach to ministry, but especially Warren Fields. Dr. Fields was also a perfectionist in terms of music excellence. He wanted our choirs to perform flawlessly and pushed them in that direction. The church, as a result of his strong leadership, was blessed by having outstanding and inspirational sacred music, Sunday by Sunday. Warren continued to give that kind of creative leadership to our church choirs. A new dimension was added, however. He evolved into being a true minister (Some years later I would have the joy of speaking at his ordination service, before he became the Director of the Music Department for the Georgia Baptist Convention).

From our emphasis on building strong, healthy relationships many opportunities came in the area of counseling. I remember one couple which came to me for pre-marital counseling. I was already counseling the young lady's parents whose marriage was in trouble and knew that she had been impacted by their relational pain. I talked with them about the spiritual, practical, and sexual aspects of marriage and, then, I asked them a question: "How do you see God seeing you?" We do relate to our perceptions of reality. If our perception is flawed or wrong, our relationship to the reality will be affected.

One day in a pastoral care class, Dr. Oates illustrated this point. He told about two friends who were riding in a truck at night on a country road. One of the friends, the driver, was from the east. The other, from the west, was riding beside his friend. Suddenly, the friend from the east swerved the truck from the road into a ditch. His friend shouted, "Are you crazy; you almost got us killed!" The driver answered, "Didn't you see that big rock I swerved to miss?" "That was not a rock—it was a tumble-weed!" The point of the story is this: the easterner's perception was flawed, and that's what he responded to.

Back to the counseling session: The young lady thought about the question—"How do you see (perceive) God seeing you?" Tears rolled down her cheeks as she answered, "He must see me as an awful person." I asked, "Why do you believe God sees you as an awful person?" "That's the way things are at home," she responded. The young lady had taken the pain she felt at home and projected it on God as though He felt that way, too, toward her. I have learned from my own life experiences and from counseling others, that we cannot separate our human relationships from those we have (or do not have) with God; they are interconnected. My challenge in that moment was to help her move away from a false god, one seeing her as an awful person, to the God revealed in Jesus Christ, who saw hurting people with compassion. As a Christian counselor that was the God I represented to that couple and to her parents. As they approached their wedding day, I observed in their relationship a healthier attitude toward God and each other.

There are times when Christian counseling becomes more complex. One day, for example, Tom Byerly, our associate pastor, brought a gentleman to my office. He sat down in a chair with a load of books under each arm. Tom introduced him and said the man had something to share with me. I listened as he shared with me that God had revealed to him that he was the Messiah for our times. He said he had been praying and reading a lot and God had revealed these things to him. He wanted to know what I thought and what my suggestions might be as a pastor.

My Clinical Pastoral training at Central State Hospital suddenly became very important. I had been the chaplain for mentally suffering male patients. So, I shared my concern for the gentleman and remembered what Clarence Barton taught me at Central State—try to guide them from the "there and then" to the "here and now" of their lives. I was not trained to deal with his psychosis. But, as a trained spiritual counselor I could, hopefully, guide him toward reality about the Messiah. For this I would need to use the Bible. I said, "Gary, (not his real name) the Bible says that when the Messiah comes, He will establish His kingdom here on earth. Have you decided how you're going to do that? Are you going to the UN and share it with the nations?" His eyes were wide open, "And Gary, when the Messiah comes, the Bible says every knee will bow and every tongue will confess Him as Lord. This Sunday, do you want me to have you stand and invite the church to bow down and confess you as Lord?" (He and his children had been visiting our church). Suddenly, Gary began to face the "here and now" of his life. He talked about his family and some of the struggles they were facing. Tom and I encouraged him and pledged to give him and his family all of the support we could. I also encouraged him to stay close to his medical support system.

With the cooperation of the ministerial staff, I led our church to develop a spiritual support system. Its purpose was to nurture strong Christians, healthy relationships and a mature, outgoing witness beyond the walls of the church buildings. The system had four visible focal points — the baptistry, the Lord's table, the diaconate and mid-week prayer and share services. We gave a name to the program — The Ministry of Encouragement.

Frank leading a Ministry of Encouragement session with Associate Pastor, Tom Byerly, looking on; FBC Statesboro, circa 1976

The scope of encouragement was the entire human life cycle — from birth until death. When there was a birth in our church family, along with pastoral hospital visits, the deacon shepherds (as they were called) communicated with the parents in their deacon zones to plan the parent/child dedication service, with the deacon presenting the parents and their children to the gathered church family. The deacons also remembered the birthdays of members for whom they were responsible. My deacon, on my birthday, called and sang "Happy Birthday" to me. It was the worst rendition of the song I had ever heard! He, like his pastor, was not blessed in the music department. I knew, however, that the system was working and was grateful for the call. When there was a baptism, the new member's deacon lighted a candle from the Christ candle on the Lords table. The candle symbolized the new Christian's place at the Father's family table. All of the significant events of life — birthdays, baptisms, graduations, weddings, hospitalizations, major illnesses, retirements and deaths — became occasions for pastoral and deacon shepherd involvement: this was the team approach I had learned in my Clinical Pastoral Education experiences.

The deacons began to transition away from being just an administrative board toward being collaborators with the ministerial staff in caring for the First Baptist flock. The communication center for the Ministry of Encouragement was the mid-week fellowship services (held on Thursday evenings because many of the business people in town closed their shops on Wednesday afternoons). Frances Smith, the church cook and her husband, Waldo, who was the head custodian, prepared delicious meals for us. Their fried chicken and fish rivaled that of the best restaurants in town. Attendance was excellent! I became the communicator-in-chief.

All the information we could gather—births, birthdays, new members, visitors names, names of "away" members in schools and the military, home-bound members, the hospitalized, church staff anniversaries, weddings, deaths, etc., was shared. Because of time limits some categories like students and the homebound were limited to a few each week. As I shared the data, those present wrote notes of encouragement. Some note writers were busy people and could not make home or hospital visits but could visit via notes of encouragement. The gathered notes were mailed the following morning to many people in Statesboro and beyond.

The ministry of encouragement, care for persons from birth until death, became a part of our church's identity. The inspiration behind the concept came from the diary of Dietrick Bonhoffer. One day the soon-to-be martyr for standing up to Hitler's regime received a package from home. His prison diary stated that being remembered from home was more important than the contents of the package. Even in the prison, he was not alone. Through memory, his family, though physically absent in the prison, was with him. Isn't that true when we come to our Lord's Table? Though absent physically, He is with us through memory of what He did for us on the cross. Then, in the bread and the wine, He is with us and we are not alone. Through His Spirit and grace and through our care for one another, we are bound together from birth until death—and beyond.

If the ministry of encouragement had remained focused solely toward the church, it would have been a futile exercise in ecclesiastical selfishness. There is, however, in the very nature of the church, and life itself, I believe, a "both/and" relational dynamic which says—"Those who are cared for tend to become caring persons." We do not become caring out of a vacuum. In I John 4:19 this concept is stated: "We love, because He first loved us." As pastors and ministers we assist the good Shepherd in loving churches toward becoming loving people. I did not lead our church to suddenly become a loving church. It had been an outward, self-giving fellowship for years, sending one of its own, Miss Virginia Cobb, who served as a Southern Baptist missionary for eighteen years in the Middle East. I do believe the ministry of encouragement gave new and creative momentum to the church's outward thrust of love toward Statesboro and the world. There were at least three impact areas in this outward movement of the church's missional care—the college community, the medical community and traditional mission efforts.

Because of the church's emphasis on building healthy relationships, I was invited to speak in classes at Georgia Southern College where that theme was being taught to students; church and college became allies in strengthening the ties that bind us in friendship, marriage and family (this was a labor of love which I thoroughly enjoyed). More college students began to attend Sunday school, social activities and worship at First Baptist. Also, there were couples (college professors and their spouses) who met for fellowship, support and discussions on various themes. I was invited to some of the group meetings to lead discussions of issues related to the encouragement of healthy relationships. One of the professors, Dr. Woodrow Powell, a Methodist, even asked me to help him write a speech he was going to present at a church meeting. He was the same Dr. Powell from whom I received an "F" on my first English theme at Furman University in 1953: how people and times do change!

The ministry of encouragement resonated with the medical community as well. A special committee, one to monitor the experimental phase of intraocular lens implant surgery, was being put together at Bulloch County Hospital in Statesboro. One of the committee's membership requirements was the presence of at least one non-medical person. I was asked to be one of those persons. Then, in the first meeting, I was asked to chair the committee. I was delighted to serve in that vital link between church and medical community. After all—the healing of bodies, minds and spirits transcends institutional boundaries (years later I would need the surgery I helped to monitor in its beginning).

Because of our church's emphasis on relationship-building and bridge-building among the educational and healing institutions in Statesboro, counseling opportunities occurred. One of those addressed a growing concern, then and now—the doctor-patient relationship as it relates to death and dying. I remember one of Statesboro's capable medical doctors coming to my church office. He sat down and cried like a baby. Then he told me about one of his elderly patients who had a terminal illness. The patient, with his family present, requested that he be permitted to die without further preventive measures to keep him alive. The doctor told me he reluctantly respected the wishes of his patient and his family. I did not sense that the doctor wanted me to pass judgment—one way or the other—about the decision. Since he was a Christian and a man of conscience, I believe he wanted and needed to unpack his feelings of sadness and regret before someone who represented the great Physician. I simply listened with an understanding and compassionate heart to his words. And then we prayed to the good Shepherd whom he would serve for many years as a competent and caring medical doctor.

Southern Baptists take seriously the words of Jesus—"Go therefore and make disciples of all nations, baptizing them in the name of the Father and of the Son and of the Holy Spirit (Matthew 28:19). Through their budgets, mission volunteers and projects, local churches support this mission endeavor on five levels—church, association, state, nation, and world. While supporting missions at all levels through strong mission giving (Southern Baptists call this approach "The Cooperative Program"), our church, and others, were very involved at levels one and two.

For example, Mrs. W.W. Mann, a member of Brooklet First Baptist Church gave a large, beautiful pine-covered piece of land to her church in memory of her husband. The church, knowing Mrs. Mann's desire that the property be used for a mission purpose, sold it to the Ogeechee River Baptist Association for one dollar. The association decided to develop the gift into the WW Mann Retreat Center. I was serving as the moderator of the association at that time. Mr. Leman Franklin, Jr., a lawyer and member of our church, and I, spent quite a few hours working on the legal documents of transfer and establishment of the retreat center concept. Then, with a few pastors and lay people, I remember a dream session we had as we walked across the property. We imagined the entry gate giving way to a long drive-way (beautiful side-shrubbery, of course) leading to an attractive and functional multi-purpose activity center (dining, seminars, etc.). We saw a lake—an essential for a retreat complex. And, we envisioned a chapel and cabins scattered through the pines, built by individual churches for overnight stays. (Much of the dream became reality and after more than three decades the gift of the WW Mann family is still serving a mission purpose).

The Fletcher family, members of the First Baptist Church of Statesboro, made similar mission-focused bequests in their wills. One gift, a house and lot, was converted into a residence for furloughing missionaries and their families. The ministerial staff, along with a few lay people enjoyed furnishing the house with furniture donated by church members. Charles Evan, missionary to Kenya, and his family, were the first missionaries to occupy the Jessie Fletcher Memorial Mission House. The Evans became like additional (and valued) church staff members while furloughing in Statesboro.

The most significant gift from the Fletcher family was a piece of land on North Main Street in a rapidly growing section of Statesboro. Our church decided to use the property to start a mission church. After the Evans furlough the mission house was empty for a few months. So, the church decided to begin a mission church in the house. A congregation of approximately sixty people met in the mission house with Rev. Tom Byerly, associate pastor of First Baptist serving as their first minister. From the Fletcher gift, nurtured by the First Baptist Church, there would grow another strong Baptist Church, The Fletcher Memorial Baptist Church. It was a true blessing to give pastoral leadership to a beautiful process of transforming generous gifts into lasting legacies of ministry.

Frank and Pat with Brad, born December 29, 1976, Statesboro, GA

In the midst of creative ministry in Statesboro, Pat and I discovered that we were going to be creative again, as parents. I announced Pat's pregnancy in the middle of a sermon; it was received as joyful news, probably arousing from pew naps some of our sanctuary sleepers. The church could not have been more supportive; their enthusiasm reverberated into the larger community. When Bradley Stewart was born at Bullock County Hospital on December 29, 1976, the Statesboro High School cheerleaders were present in the waiting room with Greg, Todd and Perri and me. It helped, of course, that Perri was not only sister but a member of the cheerleader squad. Pat had said to our children— "At forty, I'll look like the baby's grandmother." Todd, 13, had the perfect solution. "Mom, just get some of that Grecian Formula (advertised for graying men) and you'll look younger." Pat and I laughed but stayed natural "on top" (well, for a while). Brad didn't seem to mind.

There were three other events which are memorable to me about our five years in Statesboro. The first one occurred during summertime. A grandson, 15, of one of our members (I think, from New Jersey) came to spend the summer with his grandmother. She became very concerned about him and asked me to come to her house. In our visit she shared that John was suffering from anorexia. Some days he took long walks along an abandoned railroad track. Some days he ate only lettuce. "Is there anything he might do around the church, Dr. Hawkins, some kind of work he could do with others? He's so alone and I'm worried." We prayed and I promised to give it serious thought. On the way back to the church I thought of Waldo Smith, our church custodian. Waldo was not the intellectual type. He was a decent hard-working product of South Georgia. He had street smarts tempered by masculine warmth. I had my plan. Waldo agreed to take John under his wing and give him certain cleaning responsibilities. When I shared with him that John was anorexic (and explained the disorder), Waldo, chubby himself, smiled and said, "Hard work is always good for a bad appetite."

John responded well to Waldo's supervision. To my occasional inquiries about John's work, Waldo would say, "Don't worry, Dr. Hawkins," or, "John's carrying his weight." After that summer John returned to his home in New Jersey. About six years later I received a letter from John. He was graduating from college with honors and was planning to be a lawyer. He thanked me profusely for the summer job he had as an unhealthy fifteen-year-old kid. He said working with Waldo turned his life completely around. I wrote a note at the bottom of the letter and sent it to Waldo. It said, "Waldo, this letter was meant for you. You gave John just what he needed. Thanks for being his minister. Keep up the good work, your friend, Frank Hawkins."

One Sunday morning, I believe it was in 1978, an African American family worshipped with us at the First Baptist Church of Statesboro. Mr. Cotton was in the United States Air Force and had been stationed in Germany. He and his wife and twin daughters (pre-teens) had belonged to an international church in Germany. When the children were invited to the alter area for their story time, the Cotton girls, beautifully dressed, came forward, too. The intensity of heightened attention was palpable in the sanctuary. After the service, I spoke to the Cottons and asked if I might visit them in their home. They smiled and said, "Of course."

I visited them that week. As we enjoyed tea, Mr. and Mrs. Cotton shared with me how much they loved their church in Germany. I asked them how it compared to our church. They said our worship services were somewhat different but that they liked our church. I then asked if they might consider joining our church. They said they were not sure. They had told me they grew up in the Macon, Georgia area. I said, "Mr. and Mrs. Cotton, being from the south you are aware that there are different attitudes in southern churches about the integration of schools and churches. And I can't promise you there wouldn't be controversy if you felt led to join our church. This is the commitment I want to make to you: I will walk with you through the joining-process and support you if you choose to join." They thanked me for my honesty and pledge of support.

The following Sunday, the Cotton family did not attend our services. I called that week to invite them again. Mr. Cotton told me they had decided it was best not to return to First Baptist. I asked if they had received any communications which had influenced their decision. He said they had — telephone calls and anonymous letters. Most of the calls had come from African American church members telling them to stay away from places where they didn't belong. I was at peace in how I had related to the Cotton family. I did not try to make a decision for them. I remembered what one of my seminary professors said about being a change agent. He said it is important to know the rate of change an institution can absorb. Knowing the culture and the possibilities, and knowing they had my support, if the Cottons had attempted to join our church, I would have challenged the rate of change and accelerated it in an attempt to accept African American members. They decided, however, that not joining was best for their family. To push a decision beyond that point would have been manipulation on my part. I respected the Cottons' decision and wished them well.

I remember another Sunday when Dr. Pope Duncan and I had a post-worship conversation. He was facing a big decision as president of Georgia Southern College. Stetson University, a Baptist school in Deland, Florida, had contacted him about the possibility of his becoming their next president. That morning the title of my sermon was, "Discerning God's Will for Our Lives." I presented my belief, and that of many others, that God spoke to Abraham, Moses, Isaiah, etc., the same way he speaks to us today — to our minds, spirits, and decision-making faculties. The ancients, I proposed, heard God's voice not audibly but powerfully in a dynamic relationship with God who revealed his purposes and will in the events of personal and collective history. Dr. Duncan, my friend and seminary professor, agreed. He then revealed his humanness; he shared his grief as he thought about leaving a church, a school, children and grandchildren to begin a new adventure in God's unfolding will for his life. Should he go or stay? Only he could make that decision. I saw my friend and mentor leaning toward—"go." That was his interpretation of God's will for his life. He and his dear wife, Margaret, made that decision together and moved to Deland, Florida to continue a distinguished career of professional leadership. Our loss was Stetson's gain.

In the fall of 1978 Pat and I took our daughter, Perri, to Greenville, South Carolina for her freshman year at Furman University. It was a happy and sad occasion. We were happy that our only daughter was approaching her young adult years—sad that she was taking another step toward leaving home. When we returned to Statesboro, we began to face economic reality—in a few short years we would have three children in college—Perri, Greg, and Todd. We were about to face the onslaught of our middle-age years; our economic summer was arriving and we did not see the predominant color of green ($$) in sufficient quantity. And, to add to that rosy picture, I received an annual statement from the Annuity Board of the Southern Baptist Convention: If you and the church continue your retirement contributions at the current level, you can expect, at age 65, an annual compensation of eight thousand dollars. Pat and I realized our near and distant future looked bleak as in "red" not "green." Five years as missionaries in Brazil and four years in Louisville completing academic work were excellent in preparing us experientially for the demands of middle age, but not for the financial responsibilities. The First Baptist Church of Statesboro was not responsible for our lack of preparation and we did not expect the church to assume that responsibility.

I remember taking long walks in our neighborhood and praying, "Lord, we need help. Open a way for Pat and me to see our children through these demanding years." The answer to my prayer came in an unexpected manner—a letter from the Tennessee

Baptist Convention. The letter stated that one of the leading churches of that state was interested in me as a potential pastor. Then there was a question: "Would you consider a pastoral move at this time?" I had not submitted my name for consideration but was open to explore the possibility of a move. The letter did not reveal the name of the church; the TBC shared the church's identity after I agreed to consider a move; it was the First Baptist Church of Kingsport, Tennessee. About a month later I mentioned in my sermon that Pat and I were from Rock Hill, South Carolina. As I greeted worshippers after the service, a couple came by and said they, too, were from South Carolina. They were P.J. and Lorene Burns, members of the Pastor Search Committee of the First Baptist Church, Kingsport, Tennessee. A few weeks later, other committee members came to Statesboro. After having conversation, they invited us to visit with them in Kingsport.

During that visit, we met with the committee, other lay leaders and church staff members. Several weeks later, we and our children were invited for a weekend visit. The committee wanted to present us to the congregation in view of a possible call. After preaching that Sunday morning, Pat, the children and I returned to Statesboro and waited for the church's decision. D.Z. Elliot, the chairman of the Pastor Search Committee, called us that same night with the good news—the church unanimously accepted the committee's recommendation to extend to me a call to become their next pastor. Then, Mr. Elliot, leaving no stone unturned, proceeded to share with me the full scope of the pastor's compensation package (to be mailed to me the following day). The package and its comprehensiveness revealed to Pat and me the value the church placed on its paid personnel. This, no doubt, had been impacted by the presence of more than twenty medical doctors and many Tennessee Eastman Kodak management personnel as church members.

Ministers and their spouses do not choose their vocation expecting to become wealthy. They do, however, face the same economic realities as their church members. Pat and I accepted the call of the First Baptist Church of Kingsport not because of its recognition of that economic reality, but were deeply grateful for that recognition.

After saying our good-byes to the First Baptist Church of Statesboro, Greg remained in Statesboro to begin his freshman year at Georgia Southern College. Todd and Brad made the transition with us to Kingsport. Todd continued his senior year at Dobyns-Bennett High School. He missed his Statesboro friends and after a while had thoughts of going back to finish the school year. Pat and I made a promise to Todd — "By Thanksgiving, if you still want to return, we'll support that decision." When the Thanksgiving holidays came, he already had a new girlfriend; he stayed in Kingsport. Perri had transferred to Virginia Tech after her sophomore year at Furman University. Her boyfriend and future husband, Rick Miley, was a defensive back for the Hokies. The school was much closer to Kingsport than Statesboro. That was not, however, the main blessing of Perri's transfer to Virginia Tech; we loved Rick about as much as she did!

Our new church gave us an option about housing: You can either live in our parsonage on Watauga Street (which we did for several months) or purchase your own house. We chose the latter. The church sold the parsonage and we house-shopped during the Thanksgiving break while the children were home for the holidays. We moved into our new home on Christmas Eve. Pat wanted to wait until after the holidays, but the children and I wanted to be at our new address, 1504 Dobyns Drive, for Christmas. We carried our Christmas tree, ornaments in place, into our new residence for our first Christmas in Kingsport.

Janet Reece, a realtor and member of our church, guided our purchase process. The house belonged to a medical doctor. He and his wife had built a new house and then divorced. They were asking $160, 000 for the house. I told Janet that was more than we could afford. She said, "Make an offer." Pat and I agreed to $115,000. The offer was accepted. Our new house was just right for our family—five bedrooms and plenty of closet space. Its style was informal, with a Florida room and a recently built recreation room. It would serve us well and be the place of many happy memories.

I did not begin my ministry in Kingsport by making radical changes. I followed the same strategy and approach I had adopted early on in Statesboro. The Wednesday evening service became the focal point for the church's Ministry of Encouragement. The deacons embraced the shepherding concept and, while not relinquishing their administrative role, they did grow in being co-ministers with the ministerial staff in the care of the First Baptist flock. My approach to worship and preaching was less formal than that of my predecessor, Dr. William Purdue. Dr. Purdue, who retired and became a professor for by-vocational pastors at Carson-Newman College, led the church in formal worship services in which he delivered outstanding expository sermons. While not becoming a maverick, I did lead the church toward being less-formal with sermons focused toward redeeming relationships as well as persons. That approach led to many opportunities for me to minister to individuals, couples and families, as pastor, counselor, and relationship-building conference leader. This was the ministerial role in which my energies were replenished, not depleted.

Along with leading the church to become a more caring flock, I was called on to represent the church in the community and in other Baptist institutions. When we arrived in Kingsport, the FBC had already put up seed money for the construction of a retirement center for aging persons. Even though I was not a member of the project committee, I did help to nurture the project to the construction phase and gave the dedicatory prayer at the ground-breaking ceremony for the Baysmont Retirement Center.

Along with serving on the Board of Directors of the Holston Valley Hospital, I was asked to be a member of the Board of Trustees of Carson-Newman College in Jefferson City, Tennessee. Then the school president, Dr. Cordell Maddox, a contemporary of mine at Furman University in the fifties, asked me to serve as chairman of an endowment campaign to raise five million dollars among Baptist churches in East Tennessee. The funds would be used as Carson-Newman scholarships for students from the contributing churches. Our church was called on to make a leadership contribution. Don Mitchell, Carson-Newman's director of Church Relations, and I traveled many miles visiting Tennessee Baptist pastors for the campaign. Our efforts were successful; we reached the goal. Our son, Brad, age four at the time, would enjoy the fruit of our labor years later, as would many other Baptists students. Pastors are called on to be servants in their churches and beyond; it's part of the job.

The First Baptist Church of Kingsport was a mission-minded, mission-giving institution. The church, through its budget, gave approximately twenty-five percent of its annual income to mission causes. It was in that kind of generous atmosphere that one of its young ladies, Pauline Martin, was led to serve as an international missionary in Nigeria. She was more than a teacher to her students; she became a mother figure to many of them, and helped some to further their education in the United States. Pauline never married and with a keen sense of humor shared: "When I die, all of my pallbearers will be women." "Why no men?" she was asked. "If they won't take me out while I'm alive, they won't take me out when I die."

When Pauline retired and returned home, I had the privilege of leading her church to honor her for a long and distinguished career of mission service. She received the recognition with a humble spirit and, then, with a servant's heart, went to work helping others. A mental cameo I still have of Pauline is this: She was bathing the body of a young lady who lived all alone. Ron Davis, our Associate Pastor, and I went to visit the young lady who was in the last stages of terminal cancer (She had joined our church earlier that year after a painful divorce). In that hour Ron and I became assistant ministers. Pauline and her friend, Lind Willet, were the true ministers. I said to Ron, as we were leaving, "Pauline reminds me of Mother Teresa."

Completion of a Habitat house built during Frank's years as pastor of FBC of Kingsport

As the congregation was cared for in a system of mutual support, it continued to grow as a caring fellowship in Kingsport and beyond. The extension of care from the church in Christ's name into our community took many forms, too numerous to chronicle in this literary effort. One such extension, however, demands attention—the church's involvement in Habitat for Humanity. The mission spirit of our church became incarnate in this house-building ministry initiated in the creative mind of Millard Fuller. The living principle behind the church's dynamic and long-lasting participation in the ministry is, without a doubt, the priesthood of all believers. In simple English: The lay people of First Baptist Church said—"We can plan a house, implement its construction and celebrate with its occupying family its completion. The ministerial staff can help but this is our baby." We did help—driving nails and painting walls, etc., but the lay people made it happen. Over a period of eleven years, eleven houses were built; a few in cooperation with other churches. I wish I could cite the names of the involved persons. My list, though, would be incomplete; they, I'm sure, remember.

In Kingsport, and in Statesboro, I had the privilege and responsibility for supervising large church staffs (both churches had approximately two thousand members). The First Baptist Church of Kingsport, I'm pleased to cite, has become an institution where ministers tend to have durable tenures. A bit of history: the current pastor, Dr. Marvin Cameron has been there over ten years and counting; Dr. Ron Davis, Associate Pastor and Minister of Pastoral Care for twenty five years; Rev. Mitch Whisnant, Minister of Education for more than twenty five years and Mrs. Susan Hoover, Minister of Music, approaching twenty years of service. I could cite others but these make my point.

The Pastor Search Committee, however, in our conversations, had shared with me their belief that changes needed to be made in music and education. At the time, Mr. Bill Robinson was the Minister of Music and Mr. Greer Ruble was the Minister of Education. The committee wanted to know how I felt about their continuing in their roles. I told them I had never entered a church asking for staff resignations. They were comfortable with my approach to see if change objectives could be achieved with current staff members.

I worked with Mr. Robinson and Mr. Ruble for several years. They were both Christian gentlemen who had served Christ and the church well. I began to have conversations with them about their futures. I shared with them what had been shared with me by the Pastor Search Committee. I was less formal in my views about worship. Mr. Robinson was more formal than I. Parents of teenagers wanted a more contemporary approach to youth music. Mr. Robinson tried to respond to those concerns but his music identity was different; he was true to himself. I talked to both Bill and Greer about the system through which Baptist ministers move from one church to another; it is not kind to ministers in their fifties and sixties. They were in their fifties. "If you are going to make a move," I suggested, "do it before age negates realistic opportunities." Both sent resumes out. Mr. Ruble was successful; he became an employee of the Tennessee Baptist Convention in the Department of Christian Education.

The situation for Mr. Robinson, around age 55, was different. Opportunities did not come and pressure for change continued. Parents and our lay leadership were putting pressure on me and I was putting pressure on Bill. It was not a happy time in our church. But it got worse. Mr. Robinson was deeply respected in our church and the thought of our trying to "push him out" would have been divisive and could have caused a church split. I shared that viewpoint with our lay leadership. In Bill's annual evaluation, shortly thereafter, a member of the Administrative Committee strongly urged Bill to accelerate getting his resumes out to other churches. The way that became interpreted in our church was: "The Administrative Committee and the pastor are trying to terminate Mr. Robinson." That was not true. But perception became reality.

The church became conflicted. Mr. Robinson and I led worship that Sunday with heavy hearts; both of us were hurting. I received several anonymous letters. One of them said, "If anyone is going to leave—it should be you." I shared it only with Pat. She said, "I'm ready; let's leave." I knew we couldn't. After several sleepless nights, I made a decision which I shared with Pat. I called Bill and invited him to my office. Essentially I said to him: "Bill, I know you and your family are hurting. Pat and I are hurting. The church is hurting; this can't go on. As far as I'm concerned, you can stay on as our Minister of Music." He and I embraced.

He did stay on until he retired some years later with dignity and honor. It would have been unfair to Mr. Robinson to terminate him after years of faithful service once he had reached the age no longer valued by the Baptist ministerial transfer system. We then did what was creative and realistic—we called Mr. Michael McKnight to be Youth Minister and Minister of Youth Music.

The church was blessed by other ministers during our years in Kingsport. Mitch Whisnant followed Greer Ruble. Mitch was more than a Minister of Christian Education. He was our point minister relating to and guiding most of our strands of ministry reaching out to the Kingsport community. Jack "Chip" Bishop was an outstanding Associate Pastor/Minister to Youth for a number of years before serving two other churches as senior pastor-- Signal Mountain Baptist, in Chattanooga, TN and First Baptist in Waynesville, NC.

After Chip left, the church called Dr. Ron Davis to be Associate Pastor and Minister of Pastoral Care. My training in pastoral care impacted my ministry in Kingsport; counseling opportunities were numerous and time-demanding. The Administrative Committee welcomed my recommendation that we call an associate with counseling skills. Dr. Davis had recently received his Doctor of Ministry degree in Pastoral Care from the Southeastern Baptist Theological Seminary in Wake Forest, North Carolina. When he and his family moved to Kingsport, I said to Ron, "I'm probably going to resent you a little bit, Ron, because you're going to be doing what I enjoy most." We laughed. I was thrilled to have him as a colleague. I continued to do some counseling (Pat and I had six months post-marital counseling sessions for newly-married couples in our home — one of Dr. David Mace's ideas). Ron, however, assumed the role of counselor and developed a department of pastoral care at First Baptist Church, with other counselors participating. Under his leadership, First Baptist became known in the entire region as the church with a compassionate heart for people facing the pain of divorce; they flocked to our church for their Wednesday evening group meetings. Since then, Dr. Davis would go on to develop a multi-staff church counseling center. Robyn Wilson, Jackie Dolen, Betty Casey, Irv Dingus, Elaine Jones, Jean Thornton, Meri Willet, and Mary Watts gave outstanding leadership in various roles; the church was also blessed by a wonderful support staff.

Somewhere during a pastor's years of service in a church, the "pyramid-building notion" usually comes into play. Maybe it's the idea that one must leave physical evidence of his or her years of service, or, maybe it's a faint thirst for immortality. Our monument, however, would not be new buildings; it would be the renovation of our current edifices. The first sanctuary had been built in 1917 on Church Circle. The second was erected in 1927. The bottom part of the old sanctuary was converted into educational space and the beautiful wooden beams were sealed off until, perhaps, the second coming of Christ. In 1960 a four-story educational building was added. Later, during Dr. Purdue's pastorate, a new building, on the backside of the church's campus, was built, containing a gym, dining hall, kitchen, office space, choir room and children's (pre-school) complex. A wooden, covered walkway was constructed to connect the front and back portions of the campus, with the intention of converting it to brick once a third sanctuary was completed in the middle of the campus. We opted to do major renovation instead.

The sanctuary, educational space, office space and dining hall were renovated. I recommended that we construct a chapel between the two major buildings of our campus. Because of expensive wiring issues, that became cost - prohibitive. We did construct an elevator, however, behind the sanctuary to connect the four levels of the educational building. In creating the foundation for the elevator shaft, we struck water! The building committee called a meeting to discuss the problem. A geologist, invited to the meeting, told us we had tapped into a subterranean stream flowing from a higher elevation, running under the church on its way to the Holston River. Our options were: cap the flow off; that would have been very expensive; or, live with mother nature and create a channel for drain-off through the established drainage system at little cost. To this day that procedure of co-existing with Mother Nature is visible on the Sullivan Street side of the church's property. We had fun with that aberration of renovation plans. We jested, "We'll have the first church swimming pool in Kingsport, or, even better, we'll offer elevator baptisms."

My dream of a church chapel was realized out of a serendipitous moment. One day, during the renovation process, Troy Parham, Earl Dudney, Leland Leonard (the renovation project leaders) and I were walking on the fourth floor of the old education building. Because of necessary wall demolition, we were able to see the overhead beams of the gothic-style old sanctuary, constructed in 1917, and hidden for over half a century. The past spoke to the present—why not erect walls and lay a floor and recapture these beautiful beams for a First Baptist Chapel? There was a collective "Yes," and the First Baptist "Upper Room" Chapel came into existence.

The major renovation program ended successfully and one of the first weddings in the chapel united L.P. Gregory and Keith Hamilton. L.P., a very successful insurance executive, had lost his first wife, Mary Frances, to cancer. She had been the organist at FBC for many years. L.P. and Mary Frances and their children went through a long period of anticipatory grief as they waited for the inevitable.

One day Mary Frances told L.P. she did not want him to live alone. L.P., I'm sure, thanked her and asked (in jest) if she had anyone in mind for him. She answered (according to L.P.), "Yes, I do." She mentioned Keith Hamilton. Keith had lost her husband, Red, years earlier. Keith had a beautiful soprano voice and sang many inspirational solos as a member of the sanctuary choir. She and Mary Frances had been good friends for years. After grieving over his loss, L.P. followed his deceased wife's counsel and began a romantic relationship with Keith. I was not surprised when they asked me to officiate for their wedding ceremony in our new church chapel. I kept saying to myself-- "It's L.P. and Keith—not Mary Frances." Guess what? When we came to the vows I said, "Do you, L.P., take Mary Frances (pause) Keith." L.P. and Keith and family members smiled and then laughed. They were so kind and forgiving. Keith said, later, "You figured out a way to include Mary Frances in the ceremony." Not really; Mary Frances had already done that in helping L.P. to choose his second bride. They had a happy marriage for many years.

After Bill Robinson retired in 1992, Mr. Bill Simpson became the Minister of Music. He was less formal than Bill Robinson in his approach to church music. In fact, he was very open to our church developing a contemporary worship service to address the worship needs of less tradition-oriented church members. And, with the departure of Michael McKnight in 1993 and the arrival of James and Trish Jackson in 1994 (to lead the Youth and Children's ministry), the time seemed right for a "both/and" approach to worship.

My decision to give pastoral leadership to a new contemporary worship service on Sunday morning was rooted in two considerations. One I owe to Wendell Boertje who, at the time, was Minister of Music at Bearden Central Baptist Church in Knoxville, TN. I shared with him what we were considering for our church in Kingsport. He quoted to me what a church music leader, whom he trusted, said about the future of American churches in the area of worship trends. Churches, he predicted, which remain strictly traditional in worship style and substance, will continue to remain static or trend downward. Churches which become exclusively contemporary, will enjoy early success in terms of enthusiasm and attendance. With the passing of time they, too, will experience decline; the new will become old. The churches which will pass the test of time, and I agree, are those which will be "both/and" in their church music identity, offering elements of both the traditional and contemporary.

Guided by that interpretation of church music history and relying on a "both/and" selling approach, I decided to lead our church through yet another time of change, with its inevitable controversial fallout. Bill Simpson, assisted by James and Trish Jackson, gave organizational and technical guidance to the contemporary service, once the church approved it. Convincing a traditional Baptist Church to embrace a contemporary worship service, however, was my responsibility; it was not easy. Some of our members believed I was leading the church to be totally contemporary. I spent many hours with some members who argued that point. I never ceased giving assurance that the church would be both traditional and contemporary. We finally, with church approval, installed the contemporary format in the early morning worship service time. We lost a few members in both directions – some for going too far; some for not going far enough. The dual worship service format is still going strong after almost seventeen years.

The mystery of divine providence often plays a part in the roll-out of church history. After the changes in worship and music at the First Baptist Church of Kingsport, Tennessee, the Minister of Music who inherited those changes and who has given outstanding leadership going forward, is the daughter of Mr. Bill Robinson, Mrs. Susan Robinson Hoover.

After being in Kingsport for fourteen years, I was ready for a sabbatical. The church, however, had never considered that possibility for its ministerial staff. Vacation and conference time, I thought, were not sufficient for personal and professional replenishment. I was not experiencing burn out at the time, but did see in myself the signs of burn down—periods of mental, emotional and physical exhaustion. Burn down as a process, of course, will go in one of two directions: down toward burn out or up toward renewal and restored creativity. The biblical concept of Sabbath rest for all aspects of the creation is a principle we ignore at our own peril, and that of our personal and professional well-being.

The Administrative Committee of our church heard my plea for Sabbath time and granted me time off to attend the Duke Fellows Program at the Divinity School of Duke University. The decision was based on a compromise—I agreed to use some of my vacation and conference time to cover the time away. The program was basically for United Methodist ministers. Each minister, lodged in a nearby hotel, had his own carrel in the library; had his own study project; met periodically with the larger group of participating ministers for fellowship, book reviews and discussions; audited various classes, and attended chapel services. The program was designed for three consecutive Februarys. When I wrote to the school seeking a place in the mini-sabbatical program, I was overwhelmed by the response—not only was I invited to participate, I was given a scholarship to help cover the program's expenses. I did the first two Februarys (which, I am confident, delivered me from the tragedy of professional burn out), but missed the third one to address a denominational challenge.

In 1994, I was asked to run for president of the Tennessee Baptist Convention, representing moderate Baptists. The annual meeting of the TBC was going to be held at the Bellvue Baptist church in Memphis, TN. Since the convention would have its annual meeting the following year in the eastern part of the state, a president from the east would be elected in the west (That was the way presidents were elected as the convention held its annual meetings in eastern, middle and western Tennessee in rotating fashion).

The Southern Baptist Convention, as well as state conventions, had been the context of a theological battle between conservative and moderate Baptists. Each year there would be candidates from both groups vying for leadership positions at both levels. By 1994 the conservatives were in control at the national level. Moderate Baptist candidates were still viable at the state level, and, during the eighties, there had emerged at the national level an alternative organization for disenchanted Southern Baptists — the Cooperative Baptist Fellowship. Many local Baptist churches were living painfully between the old and new realities. During that period, as a moderate conservative pastor, I led our church in a "both/and" manner — to be supportive toward Southern Baptist causes while exercising local church autonomy (a bedrock Baptist principle) to be open to the Cooperative Baptist Fellowship and its emerging missional causes. Some of our church members accused me of trying to lead the church out of the Southern Baptist Convention. I did not. I was not silent, however, about what I observed as a tragic drift of the SBC toward extremism. So, I agreed to be the moderate candidate for the TBC presidency in 1994.

The pastor of Bellvue Baptist Church was Dr. Adrian Rogers, one of the principle leaders of the conservative takeover of the Southern Baptist Convention. I had had only one occasion to meet Dr. Rogers prior to 1994. At a Gatlinburg meeting of our state convention, one of our convention staff members introduced me to him as we entered the building. He said, "Dr. Rogers, this is Dr. Frank Hawkins, pastor of the First Baptist Church of Kingsport." Dr. Rogers looked at me and said, "Kingsport — I never cease to be amazed at the prosperity of the wicked." I was startled! My response was immediate — as I looked straight at him, I said, "I, too, am amazed at the prosperity of the wicked." He responded by saying, "Well, I've got to go inside."

When I stood in his pulpit to make my acceptance speech as the new Tennessee Baptist Convention president, he was seated near the front. We did not speak after the service. I did not experience either of us as being wicked. Well...maybe a little.

As convention president, along with presiding over the annual convention meeting (held in Chattanooga), I had the privilege of visiting and encouraging fellow Baptists in Tennessee, Michigan, Canada and Poland. It was an exciting and blessed year and led to our church helping to start a new church in the state of Michigan. Rev. Tommy Holtzclaw, Director of Missions for the Sullivan Baptist Association, and a member of our church, gave excellent leadership to the new church start.

Long range planners

The TBC Long Range Planning Committee met at the Baptist Center recently to consider the feedback from the committee's preliminary report given to messengers at the TBC annual meeting last November. The group, led by Gary Coltharp of Jackson, is developing goals for the six areas identified thus far — spiritual awakening, evangelism/missions, education, ministry, fellowship, and stewardship. Working in a small group were, from left, Walter Taylor and Marvin Cameron, Knoxville; Frank Hawkins, Kingsport; and Bob Polk, Elizabethton.

Baptist + Reflector
2/8/1 5

Frank, as President of TN Baptist Convention, with members of the Long Range Planning Committee, including Dr. Marvin Cameron, the current Sr. minister of FBC Kingsport.

There were two life-changing events for our church after my sixtieth birthday in 1995; one was personal — the other was diaconal. In 1996 my urologist, Dr. Mack Patton, shared with Pat and me that I had prostate cancer. My options were between some form of treatment or radical removal. I asked Mack, one of my deacons, what he considered to be the best choice for a possible cure. He responded, "I think surgery." I received much advice about where I should go for my procedure. I asked Dr. Patton if he was up on the latest and best surgical responses to my disease. His answer assured me that he was. My surgery was performed at the Holston Valley Medical Center, with my family, church staff and church family close by as my support system. The procedure went well and I had a solid recovery. Moving further into my sixties after major surgery, the expected loss of stamina was rendered more pronounced. As I viewed the next several years, though, there was still one issue I wanted to lead the church to consider — the possibility of ordaining women to serve as deacons.

For years the church's nominating committee had received the names of women to be considered for the role of deacon. Those names had never been brought to the church for consideration. The unwritten tradition of the church was an assumption that only men were biblically eligible to serve on the church's diaconate. My response to the nominating committee when they asked for my guidance was — only the church can make that decision.

I finally mustered up enough courage to lead the church through that decision. In fact, some years earlier we had run a test to ascertain the church's readiness to face the issue. The questionnaire revealed that over sixty percent of the church would favor having women as deacons. I did not believe that was a mandate for such a major decision. At the time, I recommended that we follow the Apostle Paul's counsel in I Corinthians 13 about love being patient and not insisting on its own way.

And, how could I forget that year after year in the SBC annual meetings, votes for the presidency had been razor-thin, giving absolute appointee power to the president. Asked about the rights of those who were among the 48% Baptists, one of the conservative leaders responded, "Those who are wrong have no rights." How sad! The other way of saying that is—"Those of us who are right have no wrongs." In religion and politics that attitude is destructive toward democracy. With my retirement on the horizon, I did not want to leave this controversial issue on the plate for the next pastor. Believing I had the trust and support of a large majority of our members, I led the church in a decision-making process which involved small group discussions and my Sunday messages.

My guidance had two components: one was biblical; the other personal and relational. The biblical reason given by the newly installed convention leadership, denying women leadership roles, was that Eve was first to sin. Therefore, God put a curse on women because of Eve's sin which placed them under the rule of their husbands (Genesis 3:16). The point I made to our church was this: Before the fall and before disorder and curse came to the creation, male and female were partners in shared dominion over the creation. In the second creation, which Christ brings to the old one, the order of the pre-fall creation is being reestablished. The curses on men (John 5:17) and women (Galatians 3:13, 3:26-28) are abolished!

The personal and relational point I stressed to the church was a simple image—the hands of my mother at our family table. There is no way I could ever imagine that table without mom's hands serving there. I believe that image of feminine hands serving at our Father's table was more persuasive for our church than the biblical data.

The vote was taken and women were affirmed for the church's diaconate. They have been serving well for over a decade.

Jeanette Blazier and Betty Iverson served first in 1999. Jeanette would be the first woman to chair the church's diaconate in 2013. On a return visit to Kingsport in 2007, one of the male deacons said to me, "Frank, you were right; the women are doing an excellent job as deacons." The current pastor, Dr. Marvin Cameron, has thanked me many times for leading the church to deal with the issues related to church music and diaconate membership.

OLD AGE — ACCEPTING A DECLINING ME

Autumn — We Show our Other Colors

Pat and I had passed through four of life's developmental stages with their specific tasks (Childhood — becoming an individual; Adolescence-- becoming an independent individual; Young Adulthood — finding one's basic identifications; and Adulthood — achieving a mature view of life). We were facing the onset of life's sixth stage — Old Age, with its developmental task which is, according to Lewis Joseph Sherrill, simplicity or simplification. It's the season for accepting inevitable decline. We can do that with integrity and wisdom, or, if we choose, with disgust and despair. Pat and I chose to follow the advice of Erik H. Erikson (Insight and Responsibility, W.W. Norton &Co., New York, 1964) and enter our autumn years with, hopefully, appropriate wisdom and integrity.

Our church had been very affirming in helping us to prepare financially for retirement. My health was good but surgery and stress had been factors in my reduced effectiveness as a pastor. So, in 1998, moving toward my sixty-fourth birthday, I announced my intention to retire in January, 1999. Once again, Pat and I heard the silent summons of the growth angel — "This way please." We wanted to say to the angel, "Stop bugging us; return our bodies and minds to a more youthful potency." The angel seemed to say, "That's an attitudinal thing. You can think and live spring-like in autumn, but you can't bypass autumn."

The church was packed the Sunday I retired. Reverend Lewis McKinney, a former pastor, and his wife, Frances, were present and also, Dr. James Jordan and his wife, Babs, friends from college days, as well as several members from the First Baptist Church of Old Fort, North Carolina. The choir sang a song which Pat and I had requested -"I Thank My God" by David Swoebel. My message was a spiritual journey through the churches I had served as pastor, with events from each church. The service was an affirming celebration of the eighteen years we had served together in

Kingsport.   After the service, there was a lovely reception given by the church family.   Then, what a beautiful surprise — they gave us an eighteen day European Capitols tour for each of the years we served in Kingsport.

Much had happened in our family during those eighteen years. Perri and Rick Miley had married and had given birth to three children — Derek, Brandon and Taylor.   Greg had married Lisa Blair, a member of our church.   Todd had married Sandy Lay; they were parents of Josh and Rachael.   Brad graduated from Carson-Newman University just in time to help us pack for our trip to Europe.

Pat and I flew to Rome, Italy in time to meet the other members of the Taulk Tour group.   That evening, in the hotel's courtyard, we got acquainted.   We were a diverse bunch — several Catholic couples, a Jewish couple, four Presbyterian couples, a Mormon lady from Utah, a Greek Orthodox couple, plus ten or more who mentioned no religious affiliation, and then Pat and me. In all, there were thirty four of us.   When someone asked about our background, I replied, "I'm a retired Baptist minister."   A hush fell over the reception.   Pat and I interpreted that to mean — "We came all the way to Europe to have fun and get stuck with a Baptist preacher and his wife."   We disarmed them — we had fun from Rome to London.

Frank & Pat in Rome, Italy, for post-retirement trip, 1999

We stayed two nights in Rome; I could have remained there for a week. Vatican City and the physical remains of ancient Rome fascinated me (History was my major at Furman University). We had a tour guide from Switzerland, Peter Tanner, who accompanied us all the way. But in the larger cities we had local guides with interesting knowledge of their cities' histories. Our guide for Rome made St. Paul's and St. Peter's Basilicas, the Sistine Chapel, and the ancient ruins of the Roman Empire come alive.

In the chapel, he had us to stop before Michelangelo's *Last Judgment,* and shared with us an interpretation of a Catholic Cardinal's presence in hell. He said that when the great genius finished his masterpiece on the ceiling, a cardinal went to the pope and protested the artist's exposure of the ceiling characters' genitalia. The Pope permitted him to place fig leaves over Michelangelo's accent on naturalism. When he saw the fig leaves, Michelangelo protested to the Pope. The Pope placated the artist by asking him to use his genius to paint the last judgment on the great wall of the altar. He did. In it he placed characters in heaven—Christ the Judge, Mary, the apostles, etc. Some characters were in purgatory, and others were in hell. Guess where he put the face of the cardinal who protested to the Pope? Yep, in hell! When the cardinal saw it, back to the Pope he went and said he wanted his face removed from hell. The Pope, according to the guide's story, told him if Michelangelo had placed him in purgatory, he could have prayed him out, but not even the Pope could pray a soul out of hell.

From Rome, we traveled by bus to Florence, a city associated with the great Renaissance. Then we crossed over into southern Switzerland and spent one night in a hotel overlooking beautiful lakes held in place by majestic Swiss Alps. At dinner that evening, our waitress asked if we had a favorite song for the pianist to play. I said, "Yes, Red Sails in the Sunset" (That was one of the songs Pat and dated to in high school). To our surprise the pianist knew it, and suddenly its sound was wafting through the room, out toward the Swiss mountains. After visiting Lake Lugano and Lucerne, Switzerland, we made our way deep into the Black Forest of Germany, where we stayed two nights in a medieval castle which had been converted into a five-star hotel. During the Second World War the castle had been used as a headquarters for Hitler's Third Reich.

The first night there our tour guide took us to a rustic German Restaurant in a wooded area about ten miles from the hotel. The host, Alfred, a rotund gentleman with a Santa Claus face, and his wife, equally rotund, danced each seated guest to a spinning wheel (for a quick lesson in the art of the wheel) to the tune of German accordion music. The cold-cuts and strong apple wine were enjoyable, though, even if we did have to dance for our dinner.

The next morning, after a delicious American breakfast in the top-floor hotel restaurant, Pat and I stopped in the first-floor reception room. Pat saw an elegant grand piano there and being a musician, sat down and started playing. Before long, most of our group joined us. Some of them requested songs for Pat to play. There we were, in Martin Luther's country, surrounded by an ecumenical tour group, listening to a Baptist musician, with controversy nowhere in sight; it was delicious! Later we learned that the piano was there for a concert that evening. Unfortunately, we were not invited.

From Germany we entered France and made our way to Paris. We saw the sights of the French capital, too numerous to cite, and then for our last hurrah, took an evening dinner cruise down the Seine River. It was a beautiful, warm, late-May evening. As we drifted by the Eifel Tower in the distance under a three-quarter moon, I asked some of our tour group friends (as we stood on the boat's top deck) -- "Is this what it's like to be retired?" After several days in London, we flew back home. We visited our children and grandchildren. I played about a hundred holes of golf. Then Pat and I looked at each other and I said, "Honey, I've got to have something to do." The trip to Europe and the cruise down the Seine River were great, but we knew there was more to retirement than that.

There has been more. (Before retiring I had taken a course offered by the Center for Congregational Health which prepares ministers to do intentional interims). For four years after retirement in 1999, Pat and I enjoyed interims in four churches in North Carolina—an intentional interim at the First Baptist in Black Mountain, NC, for approximately a year in 2000; an almost two-year interim at the First Baptist Church, Whiteville, NC in 2001-03. And then, after a brief interim with the First Baptist Church, Wallace, NC in 2004, I had the privilege of serving as Minister of Pastoral Care for the First Baptist Church, Wilmington, NC until my second retirement in May, 2013.

My presence on the ministerial staff of the First Baptist Church of Wilmington started, however, in July, 2004. Dr. Mike Queen and the church asked me to serve as interim pastor while Dr. Queen was away on sabbatical. When he returned in October, I was invited to stay on as Minister of Pastoral Care with a focus toward the church's homebound members. While Dr. Queen and the ministerial staff focused on leading the church toward creative and innovative forms of ministry, I became the shepherding presence among approximately ninety homebound church members. I was diligently careful to represent our chief pastor, Jesus Christ, and our church's pastor, Mike Queen, as I cared for this sizable sub-group of our church's population. Having served as pastor of a church the size of the First Baptist Church of Wilmington, I had a keen appreciation of the value of my service to our homebound members and to our ministerial staff.

Pat & Frank with Elizabeth Meyer as she celebrated her 100th birthday, Wilmington, NC

Visiting among the elderly for eight plus years, as I lived into my late seventies, helped me to see clearly three enduring life values. The first one is selective memory. As we grow older we have a storehouse of memories. Some of them are burdens and should be deleted through God's eager grace to forgive what is in our past and can be unnecessarily destructive toward the present. Some memories, though, are to be cherished and never forgotten; their energy has the power to bless the present and the future well into our nineties.

I learned the meaning of selective memory from Dr. Olin T. Binkley, professor of Ethics at the Southeastern Baptist Theological Seminary (in the 1960's). One day in class he used the term and shared with us a personal story. When he was a freshman at Wake Forest University, he became discouraged and left school. When he returned home, his mother was down on her knees in the front yard, gathering pecans. Money was scarce during those Great Depression days. When she saw Olin, she was surprised and asked him why he wasn't at school. He told her that school was not for him. The next morning after breakfast Mrs. Binkley put a twenty dollar bill in his hand and told him to return to school. Her message to him was — God has something special for you to do and it's not here but out there.

Dr. Binkley said he returned to Wake Forest and had other times of discouragement. When he did, however, the image of his mother down on her knees gathering pecans would flash in his mind and he would have the courage to go on. And go on he did, and eventually became an outstanding educator and president of Southeastern Baptist Theological Seminary. This storehouse of positive memories exists in all of us and is available for recall to encourage and inspire.

One day, as I visited among our homebound members, I found Reba Biggs, 92, sad and discouraged. I asked why. She said she was missing George, her deceased husband. I challenged Reba to go to her memory place. I asked, "Reba, what was your song?" She looked puzzled. I said to her, "You know -- the song you and George dated to." I told her about "Red Sails in the Sunset" and Pat and me. She smiled, started swaying her head back and forth and sang, "I can't give you anything but love, baby." That was their song. Suddenly, through selective memory, Reba and I were in a special place where the past was touching the present. Reba and George and Pat and I were at it again! And the beautiful thing is this — it's repeatable into our nineties — and was for Reba at 92.

On another day I visited Edith Blaylock, also in her nineties. When I arrived at the nursing home, she was sitting in a wheelchair outside her room. When she saw me, she smiled and held up some notes and said, "Look what my church sent me." Edith had received some Ministry of Encouragement notes from her church and wanted me to see them. Her main comment was — "They haven't forgotten me." At that time I was still getting acquainted with our homebound members and asked her a question about her family of birth: "Edith, how many children were in your family?" She named her brothers — about 4 or 5 of them and then paused and asked — "Are we counting sisters?" I responded, "Yep, Edith, we are counting sisters." She dug deeper in her mind, shared the names of her sisters and produced a smile of relief and contentment. Once again the power of selective memory had blessed the present.

Another value I learned as I ministered among the elderly is age-appropriate creativity. It is important for us to experience ourselves as being creative into the autumn season of our lives. Summer is over but the need and habit of creativity lingers. Mother Nature continues to be creative after summer and human nature is no different. Mother Nature knows how to be creative at a slower and simpler pace. So must we. Just as she shows her varied colors, so can we with, hopefully, a creativity less based on necessity and more oriented toward generosity, self-giving and unrealized potentials.

I'm remembering a neurosurgeon in Kingsport, Tennessee, one of our church members, who retired after a distinguished career. For years he nurtured a dream of being an artist (an unrealized potential). In retirement he took art classes and started painting. One day there was a knock on my church office door. There stood Dr. Jim Nichols with a beautiful painting. He had won first prize in an area art show competition. He wanted to share his autumn - season creativity with our church staff. We applauded!

In our church in Wilmington there are members who are showing their autumn creative colors in self-giving service to others as they live through their seventies, eighties and nineties. They help to feed hungry people on Tuesday evenings and at lunch (Monday through Friday) at the Shepherd Center; they are involved in the Habitat for Humanity program; they visit people who are in prison; they visit in hospitals and nursing homes; they are involved in state, national and international mission projects; they prepare meals for grieving families and make prayer shawls for the sick and confined persons. One of our members, Bobby Harrelson made a very generous monetary gift in memory of his deceased wife, Jo

Ann Carter Harrelson, enabling our church to purchase the old New Hanover County Detention Center building (wrapped around our church campus on two sides). The center supports and provides space for nonprofit organizations (ten currently) which offers services to people in need.

Even those who are homebound due to age, disease, or accident, become creative through their prayers. For example, one of our homebound members and I have become prayer partners during my years as Minister of Pastoral Care and beyond. Christina Price and her boyfriend experienced a tragic automobile accident when she was only sixteen. She was paralyzed from her neck down. She refused, however, to live a defeated life. In spite of her injury she graduated from the University of North Carolina at Wilmington with a degree in Criminal Justice. An inspiration to her family, friends, church and me, Christina, now thirty-six, lives day by day in a horizontal position. When she and I pray together, however, she stands tall in creative petitions for people whom she loves.

The third value I learned from ministering to aging people (I'm still learning) is the intrinsic worth of human existence. The time comes when all we have is our existence. Memory fades and is no longer accessible. Age-appropriate creativity is lost to the shadowy realm of dementia. Several years ago I knew that dementia was on the increase among our homebound members. I counted them—about one fourth were receiving memory care. They sit, stare and no longer enter into dialogical conversation. They are, however, still existing and members of families and church families. All they have to offer is their existence and that is their basic and lasting value. I learned to reintroduce myself to them every time I visited.

I remember one of my last visits with Virginia West. She and her husband, Wallace, a leader in the field of education in New Hanover County, had been outstanding members of our church for many years. Virginia was sitting at a table by herself. I sat down and said, "Virginia, I'm Frank Hawkins, a minister from your church." Her eyes moved but she did not respond verbally. She and I had had, for several years, many conversations about her husband, family, our church, and her friends; all of that was gone. Then, in a spontaneous moment I said -- "Virginia, I have a message from your church, the First Baptist Church of Wilmington. Your church wants you to know how much you and Wallace meant and still mean to us. We love and appreciate you, Virginia." Her eyes opened wide. There were a few guttural sounds and then two faint but clear words -- "Thank you." I was saying to Virginia through my presence and words that her existence mattered to her church, to God and to me.

Before I end this story about following the growth angel through the five stages of life, let me share with you some of the nice benefits of being a husband-father-grandfather-minister. I was able to be in the baptistry with three of our four children—Greg, Todd and Brad (Perri was baptized by our Brazilian pastor), and with three of our grandchildren—Derek, Brandon, and Taylor, (Josh and Rachael were baptized in their Methodist church; we were there). I officiated the weddings of three of our children (we attended Greg and Lisa's wedding). And so far, I have officiated the weddings of all of our married grandchildren—Josh to Angela, Rachael to Adam and Taylor to Chris. Through it all Pat and I have enjoyed the joys and sorrows which come to all humankind. Other than God in the Christ, she has been my greatest source of inspiration and my most truthful critic. I believe that in a good, healthy marriage two people become ministers to each other, and in that imperfect but loving mix, God brings to term something of eternal value. I have had one of the best soul mates and lovers in that process of spiritual growth.

In 2007, Pat and I celebrated our 50th wedding anniversary. For the occasion we rented an ocean-front, two-story beach house at Wrightsville Beach in Wilmington, NC (owned by two family friends, Jim and Kathy Busbee). It was a great place, spacious enough for our children, grandchildren and Pat's sister, Donice, her husband, JD and two granddaughters, Jenny and Sara. After a delicious dinner at the Bluewater restaurant, one of our favorites, we returned to the house for anniversary dessert.

I had a surprise for Pat. I shared earlier in this story that my scout master, Mr. E.D. Mullis, made a movie of our wedding reception in 1957. We had kept it for fifty years and had never viewed it. I took it to a Wal-Mart store and had it redone as a DVD document. If I had waited much longer, I was told, the film would have been permanently lost. After we watched our wedding reception, to the delight, surprise and laughter of our children and grandchildren, I had Perri, our daughter, and our two granddaughters, Taylor and Rachael, to present Pat with three gifts—a ring, a necklace and earrings. All three gifts contained parts of a large, beautiful aquamarine stone I had purchased in Brazil in 1967. For a while Pat was speechless as the family broke into cheers and applause.

We have now reached our 57ᵗʰ anniversary and are excited about continuing our romance with God, our family and with each other.

The Miley Family – Rick, Perri, Derek, Taylor and Brandon

Todd with his two children, Joshua and Rachael

Greg with his wife, Lisa

Brad, Mi Yong and Seth

CONCLUSION

Beyond Winter

Here then is the conclusion to this story and my view of life itself — **God the Creator, Redeemer and Fulfiller comes to us in all of life's stages and makes grace work in our imperfect lives and relationships.** I remember a statement Dr. Swan Hayworth made in a pastoral care class at Southern Baptist Theological Seminary in 1971. Giving credit to Dr. Robert F. Havighurst for the idea, he said that life is not lived in a straight line always going up and up. It is lived instead like this: We go up — we plateau — we go down — we plateau — we go up — we plateau. And it's in this imperfect manner that we live, make mistakes, learn and grow through life's ups and downs and plateau times.

When I heard those words I thought — "How did Dr. Havighurst know Frank Hawkins? This has been the story of my life." But, then I realized — that's not only the story of my life — that's the story of every person I have known in and out of churches for seventy-eight years. We move through the five stages of life and God comes to us and makes his grace work in our imperfect lives and relationships. The place where we see this grace best is at the cross. It is there, between heaven and earth, God in the Christ reaches out to touch our wounds with his wounds. It is in that redemptive touching of faith and grace that healing toward wholeness is possible in all of life's stages.

And how does grace work in practical terms in our lives and relationships? I believe the Apostle Paul has keen insight into grace's manifestation in the human experience. In his forever valid poem about love (I Corinthians 13:1-13), he recognizes three virtues which are enduring and relational: "So faith, hope, love abide, these three; but the greatest of these is love." God's grace, I believe, once given and received, expresses its power in the context of faith, hope and love. None of these four virtues, which include grace, can exist in isolation; they all depend on relationships and community for their essence and express their potency through acts of creation-building as the expansion of interpersonal love.

If I understand the creation in which we are participants, it came from God's grace as unmerited but necessary favor. In other words, God needed persons upon whom He could bestow the blessings of community, held together by the enduring relational virtues of faith, hope and love. If God had remained a self-contained, non-giving entity, He would have canceled grace and its power to create. His very nature, however, moved Him to create persons capable of living in community through relationships maintained by faith, hope and love, based on His essential grace. I have for years during my ministerial career enjoyed giving practical definitions to biblical words. I venture now definitions of faith, hope and love.

Faith is that abiding, relational virtue which releases powers among people for the achieving of positive good. Show me a marriage, family, church, school, etc., where healthy faith is alive and I will show you communication where creative powers are being released among persons for the achieving of positive good. But, when faith is lost or deteriorates into unbelief, those creative powers are shut down or transformed into negative powers. This happened to Jesus when he returned to Nazareth during his ministerial career. Instead of finding faith there, he found unbelief and could not do any mighty works (Mark 6:5-6, RSV). Powers existed in Jesus to achieve positive good but a lack of faith negated them.

Early in this book I shared with you about a college friend whose name was Gail Moul. Gail had, you will remember, a speech impediment produced by a traumatic experience during the Japanese bombing of Pearl Harbor on December 7, 1941. After Gail shared with us his plans to be a minister, we considered a course of unbelief but chose to be a believing community. For four years Gail lived in that trusting environment. There were no sudden miracles.

Year after year, however, we noticed improvement in his ability to get his words out in conversation. In our senior year my home church, the Northside Baptist Church in Rock Hill, SC, invited some of us (Baptist Student Union members) to come and lead in their Sunday church activities. When we arrived in Rock Hill, we had a planning session to assign responsibilities for the next day. Gail volunteered to preside over the morning worship service. For a moment we said nothing; anxiety was gnawing at our power to believe. We were afraid he might "freeze" and experience a public defeat. That night, however, we gave Gail our vote of confidence.

The next day, after the Sunday school hour, we gathered in the sanctuary for morning worship. The building was completely filled with eager worshippers. Our pastor, Reverend Lewis McKinney, welcomed the people and said, "I will now turn the service over to Mr. Gail Moul and his fellow students from Furman University." Gail walked to the pulpit and began to speak. For a moment we were tense; then we relaxed. Gail was speaking flawlessly. From the beginning of the worship service to the end, he did not fumble a single word. As Gail presided, I looked at people I had known all my life. Admiration was written on their faces. They were not aware, though, of the battle of faith he had fought from Pearl Harbor to that very moment. When the service was over we rushed to congratulate our friend. I wish I had the power to describe for you what we saw in Gail's face that morning. Emotions too rich and too deep for words leaped out at us as he said, "We did it, guys!" We had done it. It happened in a community of faith where God's grace was at work in transformative power.

The second virtue recognized by Paul is hope. I define hope as that enduring relational virtue which releases the power of the future for the achieving of positive good. One of the best books I've read about hope is (Images of Hope, University of Notre Dame Press: Notre Dame, London, 1974) by Dr. William F. Lynch. Dr. Lynch locates the power of hope in the human faculty of imagination. He writes about hope as the ability to imagine the possible. That ability cannot function successfully alone or in isolation; it needs community to move from imagination to reality. A part of that movement, according to Dr. Lynch, is keeping what is hopeful separate from what is hopeless. For example, I used to be a good softball pitcher. If I were to offer, however, my services to the Atlanta Braves as a solution to their pitching problems, that would be hopeless not hopeful. Hope begins in the power to imagine, but is rooted in reality. Some people, unfortunately, invest their hope ability in what is hopeless, or unreal, and miss their own future. This does not mean that hope does not require courage. Often what is truly hopeful faces discouraging challenges, and at first may seem hopeless.

This was true for my great, paternal grandmother. She, Lindy Sluder, and her husband, John, lived west of Asheville, North Carolina in a farming community called Leicester. One night Lindy had a dream. To her it was more than a dream; it was a vision. In her sleeping mind she saw a church house standing on a hill overlooking a valley. She identified the hill readily; it belonged to their land estate. The dream was quite vivid and left Lindy with warm feelings bordering on ecstasy. "The dream was so real; I believe God wants us to give that land so we can have a place to worship Him," she shared later with John. He gave Lindy his support but with a bit of wisdom. "Lindy," he said, "we'll give the land for a church, but before it can be built, the people of our community are going to have to share your dream." With that support Lindy began sharing her vision with the community. She did not receive the kind of support she hoped for. Lindy was disappointed but did not abandon her dream. She believed it and kept it alive in her own spirit.

That winter, in the 1880's, brought its usual misery to the mountains of western North Carolina. Snow and howling winds came at the appointed time. With them came much illness. John and Lindy remained healthy but their four-year-old daughter, Arrie

Elizabeth, became critically ill with pneumonia and died before the coming of spring. As the community gave John and Lindy support in their grief, someone asked, "Where will you bury Arrie's body?" Lindy answered from a broken and yet ready heart. "We'll bury her on the hill where our new church house is going to be." With snow still on the ground, the community followed John and Lindy to that windswept hill where they buried Arrie's body amid the solitude and silence of watching mountains. With the coming of spring, along with planting crops, they began to build a church house on the hill beside a child's grave. The church, Mountain View Free Will Baptist Church, is still there. Inside the church building there still remains the rocking chair used by Lindy Sluder during the years of her decline toward death. It is a living symbol of the power of hope and courage in the realization of dreams and visions.

In the Corinthian letter Paul states that of the three virtues, love is the greatest. I believe I understand why. But first my definition of love: It is that abiding relational virtue which releases powers among persons for the achieving of positive good in the present. We cannot love in the past; it's gone. We cannot love in the future; we can plan to love in the future (that's called hope). The only time for love's realization is in the now—the present. All three virtues, then, converge in present time. Love takes faith with one hand and hope with the other and releases the power of all three in concrete actions of positive good in the dynamic present. That, I believe, is why Paul calls love the greatest of the three. Love is where faith and hope find their channel of expression as practical, positive good. As James states it (James2:17), "So faith by itself, if it has no works, is dead"; so is hope. But as a trinity, focused toward action in present time, they are conveyers of the queen of all virtues—the grace of God which makes faith, hope and love possible in our human connections.

I remember seeing these four virtues alive in Harmony Baptist Church. When I became the church's pastor in 1960, it was a conflicted community. Unbelief had replaced faith. Faith was still resident in the lives of church members but, unfortunately, it was paralyzed by suspicion, bitterness and toxic memories. Hopelessness had replaced hope and had reduced the church's power to imagine a better and more creative future. It was a dysfunctional institution, living and re-living among past hurts. I learned, you will recall, about the church's unhealthiness in a home visit when Jimmy Nunnery asked me if I knew Pete Paquin. I was proud (as a new pastor) to answer, "Yes, he's one of our deacons." Jimmy, with a solemn face, responded, "I hate him." Jimmy and Pete were on opposite sides in a divided church family. Then Jimmy spoke words which pointed to the healing ministry I would have as the church's pastor. He said, "Frank, I hate Pete, but I don't want to hate him. How can I stop hating him?" In that question there was the beginning of personal and community reconciliation. I asked Jimmy if he ever prayed for Pete. I added, "It's difficult to hate someone you pray for on a regular basis." He didn't respond verbally to my question. I do believe, however, that he prayed for Pete.

I cite my evidence: About ten years later after Pat, our children and I returned from a term of service as missionaries in Brazil, we returned to the church for homecoming. After I spoke in the morning worship service, lunch was served outside under majestic oak trees. As we ate, I leaned toward Pat and whispered, "Look at Jimmy and Pete." They were standing together, laughing and talking about the church they loved and in which they served the good Shepherd of us all. They symbolized the reconciliation which had taken place over a decade. The church had moved from hatred to hope. Faith, hope and love had been restored to a dysfunctional, divided church because God's grace had never left and had waited patiently for wounds to heal.

What God did in Harmony Baptist Church, He does for us all as we move through the five stages of life. He comes to us in our ups, our downs and our plateau times and patiently makes His grace work in our lives. That grace, which we cannot produce and destroy, recreates eternally the enduring, relational virtues of faith, hope and love in our imperfect lives.

And when our human life stages are over — what then? Are we finished? Or, do we hear the summons once again from the growth angel — "This way please." I believe the process of growth will continue in forms of continuity beyond our powers to imagine. As the apostle Paul states in I Corinthians 13:12 — "For now we see in a mirror dimly, but then face to face. Now I know in part; then I shall understand fully, even as I have been understood." That sounds to me like growth and adventure beyond the precincts of time.

Perhaps we will be like Ulysses (Odysseus) who stood on the shore of his island home, Ithaca, and imagining worlds unknown and unexplored, spoke these words given to him by Alfred Lord Tennyson — "To strive, to seek, to find and not to yield." This way please. Brave journey!

About the Author

Frank Hawkins is a retired Baptist minister living in Wilmington, North Carolina with his wife, Pat. In reflecting back on a career of 53 years among ten churches and a term of missionary service in Brazil (5 years), he put on paper a story of their personal and professional journey entitled, Following the Growth Angel. Using the metaphor of the angel of Eden, which invites us from one growth stage to the next, he traces their lives (and ours) through life's five developmental stages — childhood (becoming an individual), adolescence (becoming an independent individual), young adulthood (choosing life's basic identifications — marriage, singlehood, and vocation), middle age (achieving full maturity), and old age (simplification — or, slowing down without shutting down). Pat and Frank knew each other as children in Rock Hill, South Carolina, dated in high school, were married in 1957 (after college) and shared a ministerial career while raising four children.

The book's content is shaped and influenced by experiences in Louisville, Kentucky as Dr. Hawkins earned his Doctor of Ministry degree at Southern Baptist Theological Seminary in the 1970's (under his primary mentor, Dr. Wayne E. Oates).

His niche audience is churches, church ministers (especially young ones), their families, and college and seminary communities. There is, however, a universal appeal from their journey, common to all, through the five stages of life!

Made in the USA
San Bernardino, CA
24 January 2016